Praise for Classe
Yooper Ale

"Cheers to the *Yooper Ale Trail*! Jon's book is a fun and easy way to get a close and detailed offering from each brewery—its beers, brewers, owners and history. The tasting of the beers is the heart of the book, and you will readily see how much Jon enjoyed each and every visit. After reading *Yooper Ale Trails*, you will want to make your own journey. Remember, you will be passing through one of the most beautiful regions of our country as you experience the many fresh brews we offer to our visitors. Cheers!"

—Lark Carlyle Ludlow, Owner and Brewster Tahquamenon Falls Brewery & Pub

"Jon C. Stott's *Yooper Ale Trails* could easily be retitled *Fun with Beer*! This compendium of U.P. breweries breaks down trips across the peninsula into easily traveled trails so that readers can take their time and enjoy the offerings of each one. Many of these breweries are outstanding restaurants with varied and interesting menus—I know, I've tried many of them. It seems that in the U.P., all roads lead to beer, and Jon Stott hits these places on all cylinders, providing backgrounds, histories and recommendations for a complete and in-depth guide to U.P. beer. Whether you are a hophead, foodie or sightseer, this is an essential book for your travel library."

—Mikel B. Classen, author of *Points North: Discover Hidden Campgrounds, Natural Wonders and Waterways of the Upper Peninsula* and recipient of the Charles Follo U.P. History Award

"In this charming book, Jon C. Stott not only provides his readers with a very readable history of the 29 independent breweries that are scattered throughout Michigan's Upper Peninsula, but he also presents these stories in such an engaging fashion that I predict it will serve U.P. visitors as a guidebook for a new 'Summer Game.' It would not surprise me, in fact, if hundreds (perhaps thousands?) of ale lovers from all over the country were to begin retracing Stott's steps. Great job, Jon!"

—Michael Carrier, MA NYU and author of 15 U.P. *Jack Handler* mysteries

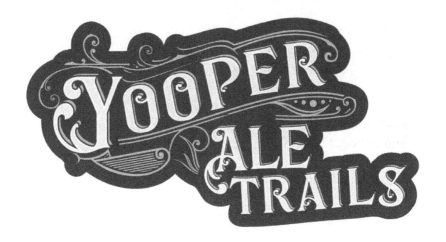

**Craft Breweries and Brewpubs
of Michigan's Upper Peninsula**

Mikel B. Classen
Jon C. Stott

Modern History Press

Ann Arbor, MI

ISBN 978-1-61599-727-5 paperback
ISBN 978-1-61599-728-2 hardcover
ISBN 978-1-61599-729-9 eBook

Modern History Press   www.ModernHistoryPress.com
5145 Pontiac Trail   info@ModernHistoryPress.com
Ann Arbor, MI 48105   tollfree 888-761-6268

Distributed by Ingram Book Group (USA/CAN/AU)

Library of Congress Cataloging-in-Publication Data

Names: Stott, Jon C., author.
Title: Yooper ale trails : craft breweries and brewpubs of Michigan's Upper
   Peninsula / Jon C. Stott.
Description: Ann Arbor, MI : Modern History Press, [2023] | Includes
   bibliographical references and index. | Summary: "A survey of small
   craft breweries and brewpubs in Michigan's Upper Peninsula organized
   by suggested travel routes ("trails"). Each of the 28 surveyed businesses
   includes brewer interviews, detailed descriptions of each unique beer
   and its composition, the story of the business, and historical
   architectural details (where relevant)"-- Provided by publisher.
Identifiers: LCCN 2023008819 (print) | LCCN 2023008820 (ebook) |
   ISBN 9781615997275 (paperback) | ISBN 9781615997282 (hardcover) |
   ISBN 9781615997299 (epub)
Subjects: LCSH: Microbreweries--Michigan--Upper Peninsula--
Guidebooks. | Bars (Drinking establishments)--Michigan--Upper
Peninsula--Guidebooks. | Upper Peninsula (Mich.)--Guidebooks. | Upper
Peninsula (Mich.)--Description and travel.
Classification: LCC HD9397.U53 S768 2023 (print) | LCC HD9397.U53
(ebook) | DDC 338.4/766342097749--dc23/eng/20230515
LC record available at https://lccn.loc.gov/2023008819
LC ebook record available at https://lccn.loc.gov/2023008820

Contents

Photos

For Clare and Alberto,
Jan and Craig,
and in memory of Carol

What joyous, golden hours we've spent
sipping on the dock of the bay

Craft Beer Comes To the Upper Peninsula

The craft beer revolution started in California in the late 1970s, adding such beers such beers as India Pale Ale, hefeweizen, and Belgium tripels, all of which were much different from the pale American lagers that had long dominated the American beer drinking scene. It reached Michigan's Lower Peninsula in the mid 1980s, but did not arrive in the Upper Peninsula until the mid 1990s. In 1994, two years after a Michigan law was passed that allowed restaurants to brew and sell beer on premises, Hereford & Hops Steakhouse and Brewpub opened in Escanaba. Five more brewpubs had opened by 1998. During the first decade of the twenty-first century, the number of openings slowed down: one brewpub and three breweries with taprooms. However, during the second decade, the Upper Peninsula shared in the rapid growth of craft breweries and brewpubs that swept the country and by the end of 2022 twenty-eight were in open for business.

Sixteen of these breweries operate in population centers of over ten thousand people, with Marquette the host to seven of them. What is surprising is that six breweries are in small towns, villages and even a two-acre private lot in a state park. According to 2021 production statistics, three breweries produced over ten thousand barrels of beer, while six produced under one hundred. However, whether they are located in larger or smaller communities, whether their annual production numbers in barrels is in five or two figures, or whether their product is available across the Upper Peninsula and sometimes beyond or only in the taproom of the brewery itself, all of these breweries see themselves as important parts of their local communities. They create, as one punster put it, "loc-ale." The personnel are active in the communities, the breweries support local charities and civic activities, the taprooms are gathering places where, in addition to drinking local beer and visiting with friends, co-workers and neighbors, patrons can enjoy listening to local musicians and, frequently, look at the work of local artists displayed on the walls around them, or at the area's natural beauties beyond those walls.

Yooper Ale Trails presents a description and celebration of the twenty-eight craft breweries and brewpubs operating in Michigan's Upper Peninsula as of April 1, 2023 (along with short notes on two scheduled to open in Spring 2023). The stories of the breweries are geographically organized into eight "Ale Trails," starting in the eastern UP, proceeding westward across the northern parts of the peninsula, often near shores of Lake Superior, to the Wisconsin border and then eastward close to Wisconsin's northeastern border and then Lake Michigan's northwestern shores to Manistique. Essays for the breweries present backstories, explore relationships between these breweries and their communities, profile owners and brewers, and, for each brewery, offer tasting notes on a "six-pack" (and sometimes more) of different beers selected by the head brewer. Each chapter draws on background research, the author's visits to Upper Peninsula breweries in 2017 and 2022, and tasting notes made during and after the visits.

Five appendices provide information for beer lovers and for visitors who might wish to include stops at breweries in the Upper Peninsula in their travels. Appendix 1, "A Directory of Breweries," includes basic facts (addresses, phone numbers, websites, names of owners and brewers), details about brewing operations (brewhouse sizes, a list of core beers, and distribution areas), information about food services, policies on admitting children and pets, and handicapped accessibility. Appendix 2, "From Grape to Grain," is an overview of the brewing process and offers suggestions for fuller enjoyment of a glass of beer. Appendix 3, "A Guide to Beer Styles," gives brief descriptions of several dozen styles of craft beer along with examples of each from UP breweries. Appendix 4, "Glossary of Brewing Terms," provides brief definitions of important beer and brewing terminology. Appendix 5, "Reading Ale About It," is an annotated bibliography of books about Upper Peninsula breweries, other Michigan breweries, and stories about beer around the world.

Yooper Ale Trails has carefully avoided the overuse of technical and scientific terminology. However, a few basic terms that frequently appear are defined here.

ales: one of the two major categories of beers, ales are brewed at relatively warm temperatures using top-fermenting yeast, and are frequently darker in color, more full-bodied and more robust in flavor than lagers. Examples include India Pale Ale, porter, and stout.

lagers: the other major category, lagers are brewed at very cool temperatures using bottom-fermenting yeast and are generally lighter in color, lighter-bodied and more delicate in flavor. Examples include the pale American lagers produced by the megabrewers, pilsners, helles, and Vienna lagers. Bock beer is a darker, heavier style of lager.

ABV: alcohol by volume expressed as a percentage, which ranges from around four percent to over 10 percent.

IBUs: International Bitterness Units, which indicate the strength of the hop-created bitterness of beer. The IBUs of lighter lagers may be around fifteen, while those of some India Pale Ales can reach or even exceed one hundred.

barrel: a standard unit for measuring beer by volume. A barrel is 31 U.S. gallons—just over 330 12-ounce cans or bottles of beer.

One final note: brewing is a fluid industry, literally and figuratively. Breweries open, close, move, or are purchased by larger breweries. Owners and brewers change. Certain styles are dropped and others added. Taproom hours and services can be altered. If you are planning on visiting breweries and brewpubs located in the Upper Peninsula, be sure to check brewery websites and Facebook pages before you go. And then enjoy drinking your Yooper ales locally, as close as possible to where they are brewed. Periodic updates are available on the author's blog www.beerquestwest.org.

Sipping on the Dock of the Bay

On a warm afternoon in late May 2022, I sat on the dock at Crooked Lake enjoying a ceremony that, for nearly four decades, I'd celebrated when I'd arrived at my summer cabin in Michigan's Upper Peninsula. The three-and-a-half-day drive over, the car unpacked , the clothes hung up, and the groceries put the fridge, I poured a glass of beer, walked down to the dock, listened to the lapping of the waves, felt the warmth of the sun, enjoyed my first sip of the season, and thought about my plans for the weeks ahead.

In the earlier years, the beer sipped was from Stroh's or Hamm's, regional breweries from Michigan's Lower Peninsula and Minnesota, respectively. But, in the earlier 1990s, after these two breweries had lost out in their quests to become national breweries, it became Miller Genuine Draft for me and Bud Light for my wife. In the later 1990s, we began to pick up six-packs of craft beers produced in the Lower Peninsula or northern Wisconsin or Minnesota and put them in the ice chest so that they would be ready for the dockside ritual. Just after the middle of the first decade of the new century, I discovered a six-pack brewed by Keweenaw, a recently-opened brewery on Michigan's Copper Peninsula. "Pickaxe Blonde" became the first UP-brewed beer to be the season's inaugural sip. Over the next few years, the first beers came from Blackrocks and then Ore Dock breweries in Marquette, just an hour-and-a-half's drive from my dock, followed by Upper Hand in Escanaba, a couple of miles closer. Then, in 2020, my ritual beer came from Munising, a small city just forty minutes away. It had been made by a very small company that hadn't even begun brewing when I'd closed up the cabin late the previous summer.

As I sat on the dock, I realized that the sequence of selections of my ritual beer drinking paralleled the trends of the brewing industry since the early 1980s, a time that marked the beginning of the demise of many of the longstanding regional breweries such as

Stroh's, the expansion of the three national (now international) breweries, Miller, Anheuser-Busch, and Coors, and the beginnings of the craft beer movement. There hadn't been any Upper Peninsula breweries since 1971, so I'd started the tradition with productions from the regionals and then switched to the nationals. However, as more and more craft breweries sprung up in locations closer and closer to my Crooked Lake destination, I chose their products. I was becoming what one of my friends had jokingly called a "loca-cervezaphile," a lover of good beer who liked it to be brewed as close to where he consumed it as possible.

The rapid growth of local breweries over the past three decades was, in many ways, a return to the ways of brewing in the mid-nineteenth century. Beer could easily spoil, there were limited ways of keeping it cool and preserving it, and it did not travel well. Moreover, there weren't roads and railroads to move it quickly and efficiently to locations away from the brewery. Breweries were located in the growing cities where they served neighborhoods or could easily be transported to neighboring cities; in smaller towns that served as business and distribution centers for adjacent agricultural and rural areas, and, very frequently, in mining towns. Beer was local: it was meant to be consumed near its place of brewing and consumed quickly. Often when a boom town collapsed, the local brewery quickly ceased operations.

Starting in the middle of the nineteenth century, the rapid building of railroads, followed later in the century by the development of refrigeration, including refrigerated rail cars, made it possible to ship beer from a central location, and many breweries became suppliers to increasingly large regions. Breweries were becoming less and less local. Only 331 breweries began operation in 1933, when Prohibition had ended. However, the Depression, grain rationing during World War II, the consolidation of breweries, and the growth of large regional breweries forced many breweries out of business and, by 1978, there were only eighty-nine active breweries (with one company often owning and operating more than one plant).

At this time, when the big were getting not just bigger but enormous and the not-so-big falling by the wayside, local breweries started to make a comeback. Making beers that were hoppier and more robust in flavor than the bland pale American lagers that were being churned out at a rate of millions of barrels annually, these little breweries were offering patrons who visited their taprooms or nearby bars and restaurants beverages they couldn't find anywhere else. New Albion Brewing Company of Sonoma, California, operated only from 1977 to 1982, but it inspired a number of home brewers and businessmen to create what were then known variously as micro, boutique, or cottage breweries. The craft beer revolution they began started first along the West Coast and then spread inland. Local brewing had begun its comeback. The vast majority of beer drinkers still consumed Bud, MGD, and the "Silver Bullet." But if people wanted something more interesting, there were often a number of alternatives brewed in their hometowns. In addition to India Pale Ales and stouts, which became staples of the craft beer industry, there were such lesser-known styles as German kolschs, Belgian lambics, and English Extra Special Bitter.

The numbers of operating breweries and brewpubs increased steadily at the beginning of the 1980s, except for a brief leveling off and a slight dip at the beginning of this century, and, during the second decade increased dramatically from just over fifteen hundred in 2010 to over nine thousand in the early 2020s. Some of these breweries have moved far beyond being local and their products are distributed across the country. However, many are very small, serving their local communities.

During the winter and spring of 2021-2022, as I did preparatory research for what my friends called my Grand Circ-Ale tour of the Upper Peninsula, I noticed that the concept of "local" kept recurring, either explicitly or directly. It was associated with the ingredients, the production, and the consumption of beer, the people involved with each, and the many interrelationships among these. Those brewers who wish to impart a distinctive taste that gives a sense of place use local ingredients as much as possible and design recipes to achieve that goal. Brewers also design recipes that reflect their desire to create various styles that will appeal to the preferences of the customers who frequent their brewpubs or taprooms. And these taprooms and brewpubs are often designed to enhance the sense of localness, of the uniqueness of the environment in which the ingredients are grown, brewed, and consumed. Often these places are buildings with their own history; frequently builders repurpose local materials, some from the building itself; and very often they have windows or patios and decks that provide views of the surrounding area. When people from the area enjoy a pint in the building where it was brewed, they could certainly refer to the place as their "Local," a term that was used describe English pubs of an earlier era.

This summer, my beer drinking experience would be different. In previous years, I'd picked up local six-packs when I found them and, on day trips, I'd generally purchase a growler or crowler at the brewpub we'd stopped at for a late lunch or dinner. Whenever I'd had the opportunity, I talked to brewers and owners. In 2017, I made visits to the twenty operating Upper Peninsula breweries, intending to include stories about them in a larger beer book. Family matters and then COVID prevented my completing that project. When I did decide to return to it in the winter of 2021-2022, I found that four of the breweries I'd visited had gone out of business, but that twelve new ones had opened and that two more were just months away from opening. With twenty-eight breweries—soon to be thirty—in the Upper Peninsula, the area was certainly worthy of a book about its own craft breweries and brewpubs.

As I sat on the dock of the bay in late Spring 2022, I sipped a glass of Three Bridge Brewing Company's "Lovely Lady Pina Colada Ale," a beer that would not have been dreamed of by Upper Peninsula brewers and beer drinkers three decades earlier, a beer that was created by a brewery that didn't exist when I'd passed through Menominee five years ago. I thought of the four months ahead of me, visiting breweries, talking to brewers, and sipping a great variety of brews, and then writing about the people, places, and ales, and realized what a wonderful summer it would be. *Yooper Ale Trails* is a record and a celebration of my journeys in the wonderful summer of 2022.

Cedarville, Sault Ste Marie

In 1943, the Soo Brewing Company, one of only four Upper Peninsula breweries to operate after the repeal of prohibition, closed its doors. After that, no beer was commercially brewed in the eastern Upper Peninsula until Superior Coast Winery and Brewery opened in 2005. It only operated for two years. In 2010, a new craft brewery, also named Soo Brewing Company opened. The 1688 Winery and Lakeside Brewery began operations in 2016, but merged with Soo Brewing in 2020. Two breweries opened in 2017: Karl's Cuisine took over the Superior Coast name in Sault Ste Marie, while in Cedarville; Les Cheneaux Distillers began producing both beer and spirits.

❶ Les Cheneaux Distillers

Les Cheneaux Distillers (photo by Les Cheneaux Distillers)

Address: 172 South Meridian St, Cedarville, MI 49719
Phone: 906-484-1213
www.lescheneauxdistillers.com,
www.facebook.com/lescheneauxdistillers

I began my "journey of a thousand sips," in Cedarville, an unincorporated village thirty-five miles northeast of the Mackinac Bridge. Until I had begun my research on Upper Peninsula Breweries a few years ago, I had never heard of the town, which, along with its nearby sister village, Hessel, has a combined yearly population hovering around two thousand. (Summer residents bring it up to five thousand.) The twin villages, located on the northwest coast of Lake Huron, had been important shipping centers during the logging boom of the 1880s and, during the first half of the twentieth century, had become popular spots for the summer homes of well-to-do vacationers from the Lower Peninsula and other parts of the Midwest. Just off an eighteen-mile stretch of the coastline are thirty-six islands, many so small as to be uninhabited, several the sites of modest and occasionally grand vacation homes.

The waterfront and the channels (les cheneaux) between the islands are the chief recreational attractions of the area. In the first half of the twentieth century, wealthy owners of summer homes frequently sailed luxurious pleasure craft to their vacation destinations. Now, day trippers and others dock at the marinas that dot the shoreline. Cedarville is home to the Great Lakes Boat Building

School, which teaches traditional construction methods, while Hessel is the home of the annual Antique and Wooden Boat Show, held each August. The channels between the islands are well populated by canoeists, paddle boarders, and kayakers during the warmer weather.

I visited Cedarville's Les Cheneaux Distillers on a sunny morning in early June. Sitting in the spacious bar/taproom/restaurant that had been created in a renovated 1960s building, which had been a hardware store and auto parts store before sitting vacant for many years, I could see the waterfront and marina through the large south-facing glass windows. One of the owners, Jason Bohn, and the brewer, Peter Duman, were finishing a short meeting when I arrived, and I had time to gaze around the spacious indoor area. There is a living-room style area furnished with comfy easy chairs and sofas grouped around a gas-burning fireplace, a bar, restaurant tables, a kiddy area, and lots of big windows on two sides. This includes a garage-style roll-up window that gives the whole place a bright, open, airy feeling. Back of the open area are the kitchen, offices, a very large gift shop and a brewery and distillery.

Jason and Peter joined me and we chatted about the creation of the brewery and, of course, the beers. Jason and his wife Kirsten Bohn and their friends Jay and Sue Bowlby had begun talking about starting a bar and maybe distillery during the recession years at the end of the first decade of this century. Gradually, their ideas grew. They would create a family-friendly place for locals, summer residents, vacationers, and day trippers arriving by land or water. Visitors could enjoy good food and drink, listen to musicians, admire local art on the walls, and relax on the patio on warm afternoons.

"This is a boating community, and so we wanted to be close to the water. People could walk down to look at the boats at the marina, and boaters could walk up to enjoy a meal and a drink," Jason explained. He went on to mention that, in just over a month, they would be opening a taproom, The Tipper Room, a block from the brewery, right next to one of the marinas. "It's the only craft brewery in the UP that has a tasting room you can 'drive up to' in a boat. We'll have the beers, cocktails and wines we serve here, along with food."

Although the company is called Les Cheneaux Distillers, they are advertised as "distillers who brew." Jay Bowlby, who, after he and his partners conceived the idea of their distillery/brewery/restaurant, had taken brewing lessons, began teaching his son-in-law, Peter Duman, the basics. Peter, a lifelong resident of the area, confessed that he knew about "drinking beer"—his favorite was Labatt's Blue—but nothing about its making. He became an avid learner, listening carefully his father-in-law, reading Charlie Papazian's classic text, *The Joy of Home Brewing,* and experimenting on the brewery's half-barrel system. "I studied about water chemistry and began to develop my own recipes. Brewing has become a kind of passion for me—and I get to stay in my own home town and give back to the community."

The beer/wine/cocktail menu, shaped like the elongated wine list of a big-city restaurant, included ten year-around offerings ranging from wheat beer on the light side to stout on the dark, along with five seasonal offerings, the most interesting of which was **Dingo Berry Wheat** (ABV 5.5 percent)—the local variant of a style found in nearly every UP craft brewery, blueberry wheat beer. This one included Citra hops giving a citrus hint to the drink.

Peter then selected a "six pack" of Les Cheneaux beers to discuss. **Buoy Tipper Blonde,** the flagship beer, is a 7.3 percent ABV pilsner-style lager. "We wanted to create a full-bodied beer for the general population. The pilsner malts create a sweetness with gentle honey notes, while the Fuggles hops provide minty, floral, grassy, earthy notes. Even in spite of its robust alcohol content, it's easy drinking." I suggested to Peter that Buoy Tipper might be called "a crossover beer with oomph!" (For the fainter of heart, there's a "junior version, **Buoy Beacon,** ABV 4.7 percent). **Moon Over Mackinac** (ABV 5.7 percent) is a wheat beer that people who ask for a Blue Moon (a Coors beer) are offered. The white wheat malt provides a sweet taste, while the Tettnang and Saaz hops introduce spicy notes. Orange and coriander notes link it to the Belgian style wit beer. "Really, it's a cross between German, Belgian, and American wheat beers," Peter told me.

Northern Tropics (ABV 4.9 percent) is a session IPA in which Mosaic and Citra hops provide the fruit-like notes suggested by the name. It is an easy-drinking, not aggressive ale and a contrast to **Island Hopper Double IPA** (8. 9 percent), in which the Carastan malts provide toffee and caramel flavors, while the Cluster, Chinook, Centennial, and Cascade hops provide balance with their grapefruit and piney notes. **Black Sails IPA** (ABV 8 percent) is a

Cascadian dark ale, sometimes known as a black IPA. The malts are very important, providing roasted, coffee, and chocolate flavors, balanced by the pine and citrus notes of the hops.

I asked Peter to discuss two beers that use local ingredients. **Vera B's Honey Brown Ale** (ABV 6.4 percent) uses honey from nearby Suetopia Farms, along with grains malted in Traverse City. Medium-bodied, it has toasty flavors along with hints of honey and bitter chocolate. Cluster hops provide floral and spicy notes. **Strawberry Basil Saison** (ABV 4 percent) is a variation of the ale served long ago to European farm workers and distinguished by its peppery flavors. At the suggestion of Les Cheneaux's chef, Peter added pureed fresh strawberries and chopped basil to the base beer to give an interesting flavor combination.

Just before I left, Jason Bohn brought me a box containing crowlers (32 ounce aluminum cans filled with beer at the bar and then sealed) of some of the beers we'd been discussing. I'd mentioned that I enjoyed sitting on the dock of the bay back at the lake enjoying a happy hour beer. "You'll have to come back here when the Tipper Room is open. Then you can sit on the dock of our bay and try some of the new recipes Peter is working on."

I said that I would look forward to that.

The road to my second and third stops of the day led due north through small villages to Sault Ste. Marie. As I passed several farms, I remembered having been told that after the lumbering era, much of the eastern Upper Peninsula had been dubbed "Cloverland" by an enterprising developer who hoped the name would encourage people to buy the land to establish farms. While some of the soil proved suitable for agriculture, much was sandy and more suitable for growing the giant white pines, most of which had long ago been harvested.

The highway turned into Ashmun Street and when I reached the intersection of Ashmun and Portage Streets, the name a reference to how boats were transported around the rapids of the St. Marys River before the locks were built in the middle of the nineteenth century, I turned left. My destination, Superior Coast Winery and Brewery at Karl's Cuisine, was easy to spot: a building that looked like the prow of a lake freighter. Restaurant patrons who were lucky enough to secure a table by the front windows or, in the summer, on the upper deck, could look across the road and watch eastbound freighters sail majestically into MacArthur lock before sinking slowly as the water drained from the lock and they again moved forward.

I'd first visited the restaurant/brewery/winery/restaurant in 2017, talking with Karl Neilson, co-owner with his wife, Paula, and brewer Brad Kent. Now my visit involved catching up with changes since then. It wasn't until October that I learned about an enormous change that had taken place. I'd written Paula to fact-check some items in my profile of the brewery/restaurant and received the following reply: "Superior Coast Winery and Brewery is up for sale. We sold the building as a turnkey restaurant for new owners to lease for a couple of years … They are not interested in the brewery. If we don't sell the winery/brewery (which will have to be relocated as the new owners don't want it) in the next couple of weeks, we will start to sell off the equipment." Paula's note saddened me. It was the first Upper Peninsula brewery to close in more than four years. I'd miss visiting and enjoying the fine food, very good beer, and splendid view—not to mention the people who made it all possible.

② Soo Brewing Company and 1668 Winery

Soo Brewing Company (photo by author)

Address: 100 West Portage Ave, Sault Ste Marie, MI 49783
Phone: 906-259-5035,
www.soobrew.com, www.facebook.com/SooBrew

As I left Superior Coast Brewery and Winery that June afternoon, I noticed a laker riding high in MacArthur Lock. It was headed eastward, as I was, and, because the lock had not yet begun to drain, I was sure that I would arrive at my next destination, Soo Brewing, a few blocks away, before it exited the locks. I passed the Soo Locks Park, where visitors could stand close to the passing boats, and the Algonquin Hotel, rumored to be haunted, and then walked along Portage Street. Had I been there on December 9, 2020, I'd have witnessed a parade of brewing tanks being pushed and hauled eastward. They were being transported (portaged, one might say) from 223 Portage, the first home of Soo Brewing, to 100 Portage, its new home. The building, which had a mural of Father Marquette, the seventeenth-century Jesuit explorer, standing in a canoe paddled by Anishinabe toward the shores of what would become Sault Ste Marie, had been the home of 1668 Winery and

Lockside Brewery, two businesses owned by Ray Bauer, owner and brewer of Soo Brewing.

When I arrived at 100 Portage, brewer and owner Ray Bauer, with his then assistant Mason Herr, was busy in the brewhouse, and Ray suggested I wait for him on the second story deck that looks out on the Saint Marys River. As I climbed the stairs, I noticed that the freighter I'd seen as I left Superior Coast Brewery was just now moving slowly out of the locks.

I'd first met Ray five years ago. Standing behind the bar at 223 Portage, he was wearing his trademark white fedora, something he'd had on in all of the photographs I'd seen of him. "I got my first one just before I left home to go to the University of West Virginia," he told me. "It was a pretty big place and it would have been easy to get lost. I wanted something that made me stand out. I've been wearing one ever since."

A native of Pittsburg, Pennsylvania, Bauer grew up drinking Iron City beer, one of the few regional brands that survived into the twenty-first century. He briefly homebrewed shortly after he moved to Sault Ste Marie in the 1990s to serve as a program director for a local rock station, but it wasn't until the early 2000s that he really got into it. "I really liked variety and I'd brew 40 to 50 different styles a year. I used to wonder what it would be like to own my own brewery."

In 2009, Bauer's employer, Clear Channel Broadcasting, helped him make the jump from home brewer to professional. "They decided that computers would be more efficient than people and so they began downsizing. Luckily, when my turn came to be let go, they gave me six months' severance pay. I had time to plan a brewery and still feed my family."

Creating a new brewery was not without challenges. In the first place, Sault Ste Marie was a light-beer town. "People were skeptical about my chances of making enough of a dint in that market to make a go of it," Bauer remembered. "And there wasn't any home brewing scene to speak of. You really need a following of loyal home brewers to get your beer known around town." But Ray was optimistic. "There were professors at Lake Superior State University, Customs and Border Patrol Agents, members of the Coast Guard, local business people and professionals, as well as beer tourists. I thought that if I could sell two percent of the beer drunk in Sault Ste Marie, I could make it." He opened Soo Brewing

Company in 2011. Soon the demand for the product had grown so much that he had to add fermenting tanks to keep from running out. His initial offerings were Goldilocks, a blonde ale designed as an entry level beer for drinkers new to craft beer; Maggie's Irish Red, hoppier than the blonde, but not overly hoppy; and Soo Brew, an English style pale ale.

Although the beer was available in area restaurants and bars, he resisted expanding by canning it and making it available in grocery and liquor stores. "I thought about it. But I like having a great variety of styles available. If you go into canning, you've got to restrict yourself to brewing just a few styles to make things economically viable, and I just wouldn't enjoy that. It would restrict my creativity too much."

So it was no surprise to learn that he'd brewed dozens of different interpretations of various beer styles since opening in 2011. In 2014, the website listed seventy-five beers categorized under twelve general categories—and the list has continued to grow. A few weeks before my 2022 visit, the website noted that Ray had brewed his one thousandth batch of beer. "Nearly thirty percent of these were our standbys—Laker Gold, Maggie's Irish Red, and 13 IPA. The rest were all different variations on a number of styles. I love experimenting—especially with hops."

His duties in the brewhouse completed, Ray climbed the stairs to the roof. He'd donned his white fedora and was carrying two glasses of his latest creation: the one-time only **Brave New World** (ABV 6.1 percent), an American IPA. The recipe included two hops he'd never used before, Eldorado and Zappa, the latter named after the musician and based on a variety that was discovered growing wild in New Mexico. As we sipped the smooth, easy drinking-brew with spicy, piney, and tropical fruit notes, we discussed the two-block move from Soo Brewing's original home.

"After several years, I began to realize that to have financial stability in a brewery, you either had to distribute your product, which I didn't want to do, or serve food. We didn't have the facilities in the old building to cook, but we did here. Moreover, I owned this building. There was room for a street-side patio and the building was structurally sound, so we could build our second story deck." I remembered his having told me during our initial meeting that he wouldn't have TVs in his taproom: "I want people to meet, to chat with each other, not just stare at a football game." But there

were two TVs in the new place: one had the computerized menu of
the beers that were on tap; the other showed a view of the locks so
that people sitting inside could watch the maritime traffic passing
by.

Ray Bauer's love of creating new variations on styles and his
desire to provide variety to his customers resulted in the beer menu
on the large screen changing every week. So it was difficult to
choose a six pack of beers to discuss. We agreed to start with three
beers that had been around for many years and one or two of
which, at least, were generally on the big screen. **Laker Gold** (ABV
5.2 percent) had originated as Goldilocks Blonde, of which Ray had
said, "I told people originally to drink one Goldilocks a day for a
week—and then have a Miller Lite or Bud Lite and they'd decide to
stick with our beer." Light-bodied and with a grainy base, Laker
Gold was not too sweet. Bittering hops gave it a slightly tangy
finish. **Maggie's Irish Red** (ABV 7.2 percent) was named after
Bauer's daughter, who, as a little girl, had drawn the original tap
handle, a titian-haired girl in a green dress, and who, several years
later, had assisted in brewing a batch. A combination of European
specialty malts and roasted barley, "seasoned" with Northern
Brewer and Tettnang hops, resulted in a rich, "zingy," malty
beverage with floral and spicy notes. The love of hops shared by
both Ray and his wife, Joan, is evident in Soo Brewing's flagship
IPA: **13 Imperial IPA** (ABV 7.9 percent). Named for the date it was
first brewed, January 13, 2013, it is dominated by the "C hops"—
Columbus, Centennial, and Cascade—which are the source of the
piney, floral, and citrus notes. Caramel malts give a solid backbone
to the brew.

While many of the other Soo Brewing beers are one-offs and
others come and go, there are several that could be called
"Anniversary Ales," appearing at specific times every year. One of
these had been released on May 10th, a few weeks before my visit.
The Legend (ABV 6 percent) is always introduced on the first day
that the temperature outside the brewery reaches 70 degrees
Fahrenheit. It's a Dortmunder Export, a lager from northern
Germany with the rich taste of dark malts and coffee notes. It had
little hop presence, just enough to cut the malt sweetness. Ray
wanted it to be as authentic as possible and found out the
composition of the water used to make the beer in Germany, then
"built" the local Soo water so that it had the same qualities.

The second anniversary beer, **Crystal Blue Persuasion,** is released traditionally on the day of the Summer Solstice. In most UP breweries, nearly all of whom have a blueberry beer, the base is a gentle wheat beer, a crossover for people who aren't ready to try more robust craft beers. Not so Ray Bauer's! Crystal Blue Persuasion has a solid wheat base, but this medium-bodied malty beer is a strong 8 percent ABV. I could taste the alcohol, which, though strong, still allowed for the subtle flavor of the berries to come through. It's still one of the best UP blueberry ales I've tasted. But you wouldn't want to have more than one glass sitting on the dock after an afternoon of picking wild blueberries under a hot summer sun!

The third anniversary beer wouldn't be ready until December 24. Called **The Gift,** nobody except Bauer knows what it will be until they pick up their pre-ordered bottles. "It's like a Christmas gift," Ray explained. "You don't know what it is until you've opened it. It comes with a Christmas card explaining something about the beer." Over the years, there have been a rye lager, an imperial Pilsner, and a Weinacht (German for Christmas) Belgian style strong pale ale.

While we talked about the beers, Ray frequently turned to chat briefly with patrons, most of whom he knew by name. One couple he introduced me to, Brian and Becky, were not only charter members of the Mug Club (there are 657 and counting) but also Canadians who had, except during the pandemic, made the trip from the Canadian Soo across the International Bridge nearly every Thursday. "It seems Ray has something new and different each time," Brian exclaimed.

The taproom/restaurant area was filling up; Ray was busy at the bar filling pint glasses people were taking to nearby tables or to the second story deck or street side patio. When there was a short break, I thanked him for his time and suggested: "If you could spend your life making beer, sharing it, and talking about it, then you'd be the happiest brewer around."

"I would be," he quickly replied. He paused and then said, "In fact, I am!"

Tahquamenon Falls, Grand Marais, Munising

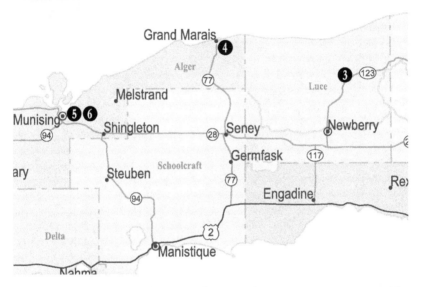

Until 1994, there had never been a brewery in Luce or Alger Counties. Then, two years after the passage of a Michigan law permitting restaurants to serve their patrons with beer brewed on the premises, Lake Superior Brewery at Dunes Saloon opened in Grand Marais. In 1996, Tahquamenon Falls Brewery opened on a two-acre plot of private land in the middle of one of Michigan's largest state parks. It would be over a decade and a half before another brewery opened in these counties. Pictured Rocks Brewery at Shooters Firehouse Brewpub opened in the town of Munising in 2013, but closed in early 2018. East Channel Brewing Company and ByGeorge Brewing Company, which opened in Munising in 2017 and 2020 respectively, are still operating.

Why after decades and decades of no breweries, did the two counties have five, four of them not just surviving, but thriving? There is a simple answer: tourism. The number of visitors who came to the UP from the Lower Peninsula, other states, and other countries, has exploded since the turn of the century. In the summer months of 2021, over a million people visited Tahquamenon Falls State Park and the Picture Rocks National Lake Shore, which stretches from just west of Grand Marais to Munising. Large numbers were knowledgeable about and enjoyed craft beer.

③ Tahquamenon Falls Brewery and Pub at Camp 33

Tahquamenon Falls Brewery and Pub (photo by Gina Harman)

Address: 24019 Upper Falls Dr, Paradise, MI 49768 (Upper Tahquamenon Falls)
Phone: 906-492-3300
www.tahquamenonfallsbrewery.com

The second stage of "my circ-ale journey" began as I drove on 6 Mile Road west from Sault Ste Marie. A few miles out of town, it turned into West Lake Shore Drive and then Lake Superior Shoreline Drive. Around the edges of Whitefish Bay were several sandy beaches, interspersed with stretches of wooded areas where long driveways led to very large vacation homes. The scenic drive ended at State Route 123, which headed north to the unincorporated community of Paradise, noted for its summer blueberry festival and rumored in one version of the legendary tales to have been the birthplace of the logging-era hero Paul Bunyan. Then I turned west toward my destination, the Upper Falls in Tahquamenon Falls State Park, the second largest state park in Michigan.

A little early for my meeting with Lark Ludlow, the owner of the Tahquamenon Falls Brewery and Pub, I parked and ambled down the wide, half-mile long paved pathway to the Upper Falls, which is the second largest falls, in terms of volumes of water per second cascading down the fifty-foot drop, east of the Mississippi River. I recalled reading that the establishment of the large parking area a fair distance from the falls had been one of the conditions of a bequest from Jack Barrett, who in the middle of the twentieth century had donated 164 acres of land to the recently created state park. He wanted the parking lot to be far enough away from the falls so that visitors would walk through the forest and experience more fully the natural wonders around them. He also required that two acres next to the proposed parking lot remain private land, which he would own. It was here he erected a building that resembled those found in old-time logging camps, named it Camp 33 (logging camps had numbers not names), and leased the premises to people who, for many years, ran a shop that sold souvenirs and over-the-counter food. Some forty years later, Lark and Barrett Ludlow, his grandchildren, bought the two acres, tore down the now dilapidated building and developed new plans for the property.

When I met Lark a few minutes after returning from the falls, she continued the story. "Barrett had been living in Marquette, but I was working in upstate New York. So, in 1990 we built the gift shop. It was basically a seasonal operation. But I felt that having a restaurant would make the perfect finish to a visit to the falls, be it in any of the four seasons. I'd learned about the craft beer industry that was beginning to grow across the country and thought that being able to offer dinners the craft beer brewed a few dozen feet away from where they were eating would cap the experience." With the help of "Chumley" Anderson, the brewer at Marquette Harbor Brewing at the Vierling Restaurant in Marquette, she began brewing on a 10-barrel brewing system that had been built in Hungary.

Tahquamenon Falls Brewery and Pub opened in December 1996. "I remember going around the restaurant with a tray loaded with little glasses of Falls Tannin American Red, our first beer, and offering samples to the diners. Some of them were puzzled; it was the first craft beer they'd ever had."

"We've come a long way since 1990," Lark remarked, looking around her. At one end of the large dining room stood a stone-faced, wood-burning fireplace. The log walls were adorned with pictures, maps, and skins of wild animals that had been hunted during logging days. Behind the stand up bar gleamed the four serving tanks that held the beers that capped the Tahquamenon Falls experience.

Although she owns and manages the restaurant, Lark seems most proud of her role as what she referred to as "Brewster," a term applied long ago to women brewers in Europe. "We make our beers lighter and less hoppy than you would find in a lot of other places. We have visitors from all over the world and we have to please a wide range of palates. The beer is a complement to the food. After many years, the brewpub is a destination, second, of course, to the park and the falls."

She waxed almost poetic about the water used to make the beer, calling it "a brewer's dream." At that point she went over to the bar and poured me a large glass of it. It tasted very good, with no traces of chemicals. "It comes from our own eighty-foot well. If this were city water, we'd have to do all sorts of things to get rid of chemicals that could ruin the beer."

Eight beers are made from this water, four of which are on tap at any given time. "I work with the recipes that came with the equipment, but I have tinkered with them over the years." At the time of my visit, the four on tap were Wolverine Wheat Ale, Birdseye Maple Amber, Porcupine Pale Ale, and Black Bear Stout. **Wolverine Wheat Ale** is a Belgian style wit, which uses Saaz hops to give it a little zing. It serves as the base beer for the fruit beers offered at various times of the year, including the very popular **Blueberry Wheat Beer.** "Chumley and I made it originally to celebrate the August blueberry festival in Paradise. Now we brew it as often as we can." Other fruit beers have included Raspberry, Peach, and Cherry. **Porcupine Pale Ale** (ABV 5.0 percent) is an English-style ale, with earthy malt tones balanced by spicy, floral notes contributed by the East Kent Golding hops. It is replaced in the autumn by **Falls Tannin Red** (ABV 5.0 percent) which is named after the rusty color of the Tahquamenon River. It is an American-style red ale that uses Munich malts to give a sweet, biscuit taste that is balanced by the spicy, floral qualities of the Willamette and Liberty hops. **Black Bear Stout** is advertised as a Guinness-style dry stout. A combination of dark malts gives a coffee taste to the ale, while Perle hops add spicy, pepper, and evergreen notes. **Birdseye Maple Amber,** a spring offering, uses recently harvested maple syrup. The beers also serve as ingredients in some of the restaurant's menu items: the stout in barbecue sauce and the wit in beer cheese soup and beer cheese spread. There's a beer batter for the white fish entrees.

I noted that the parking lot had begun to fill up and remarked that I'd better leave, giving Lark the time to prepare for the people who would soon be coming through the doors: "Do you ever wish you could get away from it all and take a rest? You're in the middle of the woods, but you're surrounded by people nearly every day."

She responded enthusiastically: "I've been doing this for a quarter of a century. I still love it. And it's fun to know that I was the first craft beer brewster in the UP."

④ Lake Superior Brewing Company at Dunes Saloon

Lake Superior Brewing Company (photo by author)

Address: N 14283 Lake Ave, Grand Marais, MI 49839
Phone: 906-494-2337
www.grandmaraismichigan.com/lsbc
www.facebook.com/LakeSuperiorBrewing

In traveling from Upper Tahquamenon Falls to Grand Marais, the shortest route is County Road 37, which heads northwest off of Michigan 123 approximately ten miles north of Newberry. However, portions of the road are gravel and cell-phone reception is iffy. I usually proceed southwest down 123 until I reach Michigan 28—the major east-west road across the northern Upper Peninsula—and then head west twenty-two miles to Seney and then north on Michigan 77 to Grand Marais. This route lacks the scenic grandeur of 37, but passes some significant historical spots. On the northern outskirts of Newberry is the Tahquamenon Logging Museum, well worth an hour stop to look at pictures from the logging era as well as tools used by the loggers. There's a gift shop and, if you're around on Saturday mornings during the summer, you can enjoy a traditional loggers' breakfast. Seney is now just a four-corners, but in the late nineteenth century, it was one of the "hell-towns in the pines." At the end of the winter logging season, men from the camps used to descend on the town, determined to spend as much of their pay as they could at the town's saloons and brothels. The drive north is through country described by Ernest Hemingway in his famous early 1920s short-story "Big Two-Hearted River." From the hill above Grand Marais, a village with a year-around population of just under three hundred, but a summer one of nearly two thousand, you can see Lake Superior extending north into the distance. The village, which looks like a fishing town on the coast of Maine, was home to over a dozen lumber mills during the logging era.

Lake Superior Brewing Company at the Dunes Saloon is housed in a long, narrow building with the parking lot on one side filled with motorcycles (the winding County Road 58 that heads west is a favorite with cyclists) and many cars with out-of-state license plates. The front room houses the bar, which dispenses a full range of liquor, wines and beer, including cans of Miller, Budweiser, and Coors. Shelves of bottles front the full mirror; there is a large TV, a pool table and a juke box. Perhaps the most interesting features of the room are the barrel-shaped tables, each topped with a large sliced and polished piece of agate under glass. (The area is a favorite spot for collectors of these semi-precious stones.)

A narrow corridor leads into the back dining room, which contains more of the barrel/agate tables and along one wall, behind floor-to-ceiling glass, the 5.5 barrel brewing system. It had come from a brewery in Slidell, Louisiana and had been made largely out of old dairy tanks. A visitor to Grand Marais had told Dave Beckwith, the first brewer and now brewpub general manager, that the southern brewery was upgrading and that its tanks were for sale. "We bought them; the owner/brewer delivered them and then gave us a one-day crash course in brewing. He provided us with six recipes and then left," Dave told me when I first visited Dunes in 2017. "We videotaped the proceedings and it's lucky that we did. We had to play the tape quite a few times after he'd left and we were on our own."

During my 2017 visit, Beckwith reminisced about his life as a "pioneer brewer" working at the second oldest brewpub in the Upper Peninsula. (Escanaba's Hereford & Hops had opened just a few months before Lake Superior Brewing began operations in late

1994.) He'd grown up in nearby Munising, where his family was in the restaurant business, and had moved to Grand Marais in the early 1990s to run the kitchen at the Sportsman's Restaurant. "When Chris Sarver decided to open a new restaurant, he asked if I would come and run his kitchen. I'd been hearing about brewpubs opening up in Michigan and I told him that I would if somebody would teach me how to brew beer." Sarver agreed and Dave, who until that time had been a Blatz and Pabst Blue Ribbon drinker, took his one-day crash course and entered the world of craft brewing.

"The brewer from Louisiana who helped us set up the equipment suggested that we start with an amber ale, which he said was fairly simple to make and would appeal to a wide range of drinker. We called it Agate Amber. But neither Chris nor I liked it, so we replaced it with an ESB [Extra Special Bitter]. It took a while to get the locals used to the new kinds of beer, and many of them stuck with the bottled beer. We developed six regular brews. We wanted everyone to have something that they could call their favorite."

In addition to playing a pioneer role in Upper Peninsula brewing, Dave Beckwith also became a character in some of the Upper Peninsula stories of well-known novelist Jim Harrison. He's "Dave the Bartender." During the many springs, summers, and autumns that the author was at his nearby cabin at the edge of the Sucker River, he spent many evenings at the Dunes Saloon. He didn't have a telephone at his cabin and his editor would phone the Dunes and leave messages. After his writing day was over, he'd drive his truck to the village, enter the brewpub, and use the telephone to reply to messages left on a clipboard next to the kitchen. "It was a wall phone with a long cord and while he was talking he'd wander over to the freezer, take out a frozen hamburger patty and put it in his pocket," Beckwith remembered. "When he'd finished his business, he'd take the hamburger out to his dog, who was sitting in the truck, and then come back in to eat and drink. He'd hold court; as the evening went on, more and more people would wander over to his table. Some of them didn't even know who he was; but they loved his stories."

During my 2017 visit, I met Sean DeWitt, who had recently taken over brewing duties. Beckwith's role as general manager of Dunes had taken most of his time and he had initially turned over his duties to Robert Nyman, who had suggested that DeWitt take over when he decided to move on. A troll (that's Yooper slang for someone who lives "under the bridge" that is in the Lower Peninsula, below the Mackinac Bridge), he'd never tasted craft beer until he first visited Grand Marais with his then girlfriend, now wife, Andrea. "We went to the Dunes and I had a Sandstone Pale Ale. I'd never had anything so good. Working on cars in Detroit was just a job," he said, the enthusiasm in his voice increasing as he continued. "But after only a few months, brewing has become a passion. I'm in a town where I want to live and making beer that people like."

When I visited DeWitt again in early June 2022, he talked about his five years as a brewer. The passion was still as strong as ever, he told me. "And I've learned so much. I've learned about the diverse styles and I've developed a much more discerning palate. With so many tourists who know a lot about craft beer stopping here, I really have to be aware of changes and new trends."

We discussed "a six-pack" of Lake Superior Brewing's beers. Sean noted that several of the originals were still regularly on tap and that, although he's done some tinkering with the recipes. **Blonde Ale** is still the crossover beer. Low in alcohol (ABV 4.5 percent), it is light-bodied, with the Tettnang hops adding lightly spicy notes. **Puddingstone Wheat** (ABV 4.2 percent) is another beer designed as an introductory craft ale. Low in hops, it has a creamy mouthfeel, and a clean finish. **Sandstone Pale Ale** (ABV 5.5 percent) is the brewery's flagship ale. An American-style pale ale, it has citrusy and piney notes. **Granite Brown** (ABV 5.4 percent) is another of the original beers. Caramel and chocolate malts give it a full-bodied roasty taste. It's low in bitterness. **Hindsight Double IPA** (ABV 8 percent) is Lake Superior Brewing's heavy hitter. It's a very hoppy beer, with Citra, Amarillo, and Cascade hops that provide strong citrus notes that are balanced by the slight sweetness of the pale malts.

The sixth beer Sean talked about was the one that, he said, "I feel best about. I've worked hard at it." It's **First Creek Kolsch** (ABV 5.2 percent), a German style ale that probably wasn't known to most of the people who first sampled craft beer at the Dunes in 1994. A clean, refreshingly crisp beer that some people have called "the ale that wants to be a lager," it is now made by many Upper Peninsula brewers, who enjoy the challenges of engaging with the style and of presenting new craft beer drinkers with a more subtle, but approachable crossover beer. The spiciness of the Hallertau hops balances the slightly sweet, bready quality of the pilsner malts.

When I asked Sean if he had any time to enjoy the passions of hunting and fishing that first drew him to the area, he replied, "Not until after Labor Day. The tourist season is just beginning now and so I'll be indulging my third passion, brewing, nearly every day. It takes twenty-one days to complete the process of brewing a beer and eighteen days for the people to drink it. But I'm not complaining. I get paid to brew; but it's really a labor of love."

⑤ East Channel Brewing Company

East Channel Brewing Company(photo by author)

Address: 209 Maple St., Munising, MI 49862
Phone: 906-387-3007
www.eastchannelbrewery.com,
www.facebook.com/EastChannelBrew

Along the first twelve miles of the winding County Road 58 from
Grand Marais to Munising are two or three scenic pull-offs offering
striking views of Lake Superior. One of the most interesting is at
Hurricane River Campground, where a mile-and-a-half, pedestrian-
only dirt road bordering the shore line leads to the historic Au Sable
Light Station. Along the way are signs pointing toward the sandy
beach indicating the locations of the remains of boats wrecked over
a century ago. Close to Munising, a road leads off to Miners Castle,
a scenic overlook of the Pictured Rocks. Coming into the town of
just over 2,000 people, County road 58 passes one of the mills that
has provided the major source of income for a large number of the
residents. While the mill still operates, tourism has also become an
extremely important "industry" for the area. Two new craft breweries play not insignificant roles in that industry.

East Channel Brewing, which is named after the stretch of water between the eastern shore of Grand Island and the mainland, began serving its beer in 2016. It is situated just over three blocks from the departure point for the Pictured Rocks boat cruises in a small building that has housed a horse stable, a sign shop, a glass factory, and, most recently, district social services offices. On the lower floor of the taproom on a shelf overlooking the bar is a life-size carving of Itchee, the seagull mascot who is pictured on all of the can labels. Refinished floors and wall paneling give the place the dark and comfortable look of a "snug," an English pub where locals could enjoy a pint at the end of the day. Behind the taproom stands the 3.5 barrel brewhouse. The upper story is much brighter, as full windows look out onto the street and let in cheery sunshine. Pew-like benches along the walls and a table piled with board games enhance the English pub feel. The cozy atmosphere is what co-owners Joe DesJardins and Ted Majewski intended. "We wanted something for locals who were looking for a quiet place to unwind, relax and have a quiet conversation," Joe told me when I first visited East Channel in the late spring of 2017. "This is about craft beer and it's for the people who enjoy it. We welcome tourists, but we are here for the locals."

DesJardins and Majewski had met when Ted began dating Joe's sister. Joe, a home brewer, convinced Ted that the hobby could be very interesting. The two had different tastes in beer. Although both were fans of Bell's Brewery of Kalamazoo, Joe's favorite was Two Hearted Ale, a big, hoppy beer; Ted's, the rich, malty Best Brown. When they opened East Channel in 2016, their beer list reflected this diversity. "We wanted to give people a range of colors, a range from light to full-bodied, and a range from lower to higher alcohol," Joe, who handles most of the brewing, explained.

When they opened, they installed a small canning machine behind the bar. It was capable filling two cans a minute and was intended as a service for in-house patrons who wanted to take some of the beers they enjoyed back to their homes, motels, or campsites. After a year or two, they installed a new one capable of filling eight cans a minute, so that they could supply six packs to local grocery and party stores. Now, Joe told me, they had purchased one that could fill thirty to fifty cans a minute. It would be part of a planned twenty-barrel facility that would produce enough beer for them to distribute across the Upper Peninsula.

Tourists are still very welcome at the East Channel tap room. "But we're still very much here for the locals. They have become very knowledgeable about the various craft brew styles and are often making suggestions to us." Joe said that the brewery is part of two communities: the community in which they live and the community of craft brewers. "Four years after we opened, ByGeorge started up just a couple of blocks away. We work together as brewers and we often sponsor community events together."

Joe described the house style as beers that are approachable. "We have the familiar range of craft beers and we try to avoid making any of them too bitter." One that was at the high end of bitterness and strength, at 7.6 percent ABV and 90 IBUs is **Old Tru IPA**, named after DesJardin's great-great-grandfather, a Munising pioneer who grew hops. The label declares that it's "an IPA like the man ... simple and honest." Based on one of Joe's homebrew recipes, it is hop-forward, with the mix of Amarillo, Mosaic, Falconer's Flight, Citra, Warrior, and Simcoe hops supplying fruity, piney, citrusy, and herbal flavors, along with a bracing bitterness. At the other end of the spectrum is **Paradise Waitin' Blueberry Lager** (ABV 4 percent), East Channel's take on the Upper Peninsula's most popular style. "It's like a pilsner," DesJardins said. "There are pils malts, honey malts, and flaked rice to give it a gentle malt backbone, Saaz hops provide a crisp, clean spiciness, and a hint of blueberry.

Hobo Nectar Lager (ABV 4.6 percent) is the brewery's crossover beer. Light-bodied, it has a spicy hoppiness, a gentle malt background, and crisp finish. **Island's Grand as Always Blood Orange Hefeweizen** (ABV 5 percent) is about summer in two ways: the name of the beer comes from Joe's father's saying about warm afternoons finishing around nearby Grand Island, and the light-bodied hefeweizen infused with blood orange puree is a fine summer afternoon thirst-quencher. The pilsner malts give it a light body and the red wheat malt the distinctive taste of a favorite German style. **Lake Street Stout** (ABV 5.7 percent) is East Channel's way of saying, "Don't be afraid of the Dark." An oatmeal stout, it doesn't have the overly roasty flavors of many stouts, and finishes clean and crisp. "It's very light-bodied for a stout," DesJardins explained.

⑥ ByGeorge Brewing Company

ByGeorge Brewing Company (photo by author)

Address: 231 East Superior St, Munising MI, 49862
Phone: 906-387-2739
www.bygeorgebrewing.com
www. facebook.com/bygeorgebrewing

In 2018, when Pictured Rocks Brewing ceased operations after only five years, many people wondered if Munising, with a population of less than three thousand, was too small to support two craft breweries. But, by George, they were wrong. Just over two years later, another brewery opened. ByGeorge Brewing began business in late January 2020, just weeks before the onslaught of the corona virus in Michigan. Located two blocks from East Channel, it made Munising one of three Upper Peninsula cities where craft beer loving patrons could walk from one to another taproom. (The other two are Marquette, and Houghton.) Although business at the two breweries was severely restricted in 2020, both have not only survived, but also have grown.

ByGeorge Brewing plays on the expression of surprise (and some of the brews may elicit surprise) and the name of one of the co-owners, George Schultz. He and his partner, Matt Johnson, are both Munising residents who became friends through their interest in home brewing. Schultz had been home brewing since early in this century, had made his first batch of beer from a kit, and then began experimenting, developing his own recipes and brewing a wide range of styles—beers that weren't available in the Upper Peninsula. He had a four-tap setup in his basement recreation room and invited friends (many of them also home brewers) to try his newest creations. "We'd discuss each beer and in that way we increase our knowledge of craft beer styles."

Schultz was always glad to share his growing knowledge of craft beer and brewing, a knowledge he said was in part grounded in his university studies of chemistry, part of the pharmacy program he was enrolled in at Ferris State University in Michigan's Lower Peninsula. Like many home brewers, Schultz wanted to start his own brewery. At one point, he considered opening one in Christmas, a nearby hamlet, and calling it "Rudolph the Red." "But the banks thought that granting a loan for a brewery was too risky." Then, when his employer, Snyder's Drugs, closed its Munising store and he found himself unemployed, he decided the time was right to try again. He asked his friend Matt Johnson, who was part of a well-known construction company in the area, to join him. George, with his wife, Amber, owned a building on Munising's main street and, with Matt as his partner, converted the building, which had housed a flower shop, among other businesses, into a deli restaurant (owned and run by his wife), a brewery, and a taproom. "Matt handled the renovations and I began to set up the brewhouse and devise recipes. Matt is so well organized in all details of running the business; he keeps everything shipshape and running. I play around with ideas; he makes sure we all have our feet on the ground."

"Our first beer was a dry Irish stout," Schultz recalled. "It was based on a home-brew recipe I'd been tinkering with for quite a while and it was a good recipe to test out how well Munising's water worked in brewing. We made it a lower-alcohol session beer that would be a good introduction for people new to craft beers." He also offered the standard craft styles, including IPAs, along with some "crazy recipes such as a chocolate, peanut butter porter."

When I first entered the taproom of ByGeorge brewing, I quickly noticed something different from other taprooms. Instead of a chalkboard or a TV screen listing the various beers, the wall above the tap handles was decorated with large, colorful illustrated posters, one for each of the beers currently available. "We have them done by local artists; it's a way of involving the community and it's an entertaining way of letting our customers know what's available." Two particularly caught my eye. The Big Cups Peanut Butter and Dark Chocolate Porter showed an animated chocolate cup, holding a top hat in a white gloved hand. In the background floated peanuts in the shell and chocolate chips. Blueberry and Maple Pancake Pilsner depicted a maple syrup bottle pitching a blueberry at a pancake-headed batter swinging a flapjack flipper.

Shultz described six of ByGeorge's beers, going from the light to the dark and then finishing with one of his unusual "creations." **Walking with Giants** (ABV 4.7 percent) is an apricot-flavored blonde ale. Designed as a gentle crossover beer for craft beer novices, it combines the smooth, easy-drinking qualities of a blonde ale with hints of apricot aroma and flavor. Since ByGeorge began canning in the spring of 2022, it has become the brewery's second-bestselling packaged brew. **Maize 'n' Grace** (ABV 4.1 percent), the number three best-seller in cans, is described by Schultz as "a craft twist on the thirty-pack lager so popular with drinkers of mainstream beers. Flaked maize contributes a slightly sweet flavor, while crystal and centennial malts provide a crisp, clean balance with a hop tang. It's a refreshing and sessionable light-bodied lager.

Elephant Disco IPA (ABV 6.8 percent) is one of two regularly available IPAs offered by ByGeorge. The top-seller in cans, it's an American style IPA, with the piney and citrusy notes of the Warrior and Veteran's Blend hops balanced by a malty background. "It's a smooth, balanced and not aggressive beer," Schultz remarked. From elephants to unicorns is quite a jump, but the brewery does this successfully in the zanily-named **Unicorn Piss**, a 6.6 percent ABV New England style IPA. It, like Elephant Disco, is not aggressive although Citra, Amarillo, and Azacca hops provide a range of citrusy flavors from slightly tart to sweet. The malt base provides a medium-bodied balance to the hop flavors.

In a locality where the light version of a mass-produced pale American lager is the top selling beer, it may be surprising that many Upper Peninsula craft brewers report that dark beers such as stouts and schwarzbiers are among their more popular offerings. This is the case with ByGeorge's **Nighthawk Onyx Ale** (ABV 4.5

percent), a dark beer that has been compared to a German schwarzbier and an English stout. "We named it an onyx ale to pique people's curiosity. Deep brown/black and opaque, it is a toasty beer that uses roasted black barley to give it a rich flavor. It finishes clean and is fairly light-bodied. We call it the beer with a dark body and blonde soul," Schultz said with a laugh.

The final beer we talked about represented the wild, creative styles ByGeorge is becoming noted for along with its classic renditions of traditional styles. It's an IPA, but not your traditional West Coast-style IPA, although it has some bitterness. It's a New England-style IPA, fuller-bodied and sweeter than its cross-continent cousin. But it's even fuller-bodied than that. The addition of milk sugar makes it thicker, creamier and smoother than the usual New England version. And, in addition to the tropical fruit notes of the hops, it has strawberry flavors. This is a summer beer, but no lawnmower light lager. Its name: **Leader of the Patch: Strawberry Milkshake IPA** (ABV 7.3 percent).

While George was describing and I was sipping from a sample glass, I looked up above the taps and spotted the poster for this very different ale. A fierce-looking motorcycle gang roared down both sides of a two-lane road. In the front were three tough looking strawberries; behind them a group of milk bottles. I chuckled and remembered what Schultz had said earlier in our conversation: "We take brewing beer very seriously; but not ourselves."

Harvey, Marquette
(lakeside)

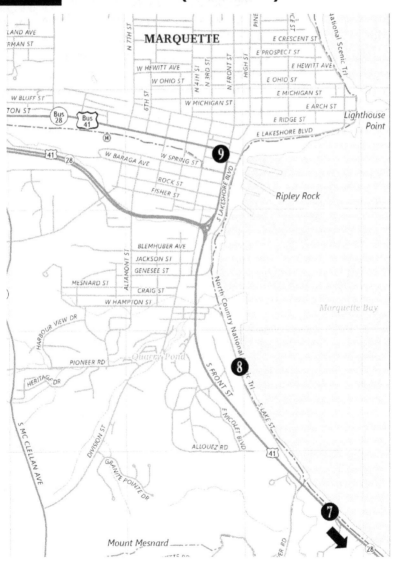

Along the forty-two mile stretch of Michigan Highway 28 between Munising and downtown Marquette, there are several scenic rest areas where travelers can park and gaze at the waters of Lake Superior (which is sometimes fairly calm, but not infrequently roiling with high, white-crested waves hurling themselves onto the sand). The highway joins US Highway 41 on the last four miles into Michigan and passes close by three breweries located to the east of the highway and to the west of the North Country Trail, which skirts the shores of the big lake. Lake Superior Smokehouse Brewpub, the southernmost of these, located in the Marquette suburb of Harvey, and Drifa Brewing, situated at the southern edge of downtown, both opened in 2019. The most northern, Marquette Harbor Brewing Company at Vierling Restaurant, which began brewing in 1995 and is the third-oldest craft brewery in the Upper Peninsula, is on the western edge of downtown and overlooks the Lower Harbor and the now decommissioned Lower Harbor Ore Dock.

⑦ Lake Superior Smokehouse Brewpub

Lake Superior Smokehouse Brewpub (photo by author)

Address: 200 West Main St, Harvey, MI 49855
Phone: 906-273-0952
www.lakesuperiorsmokehouse.com
www.facebook.com/lakesuperiorsmokehousepub.com

Situated just a block from the North Country Trail and the estuary of the Chocolay River, the Smokehouse Brewpub occupies the building that had been the home of Bayou Bar and Grille and Chocolay River Brewery until it closed suddenly in the summer of 2017, leaving some of the tanks half full of recently brewed beer. Scott Arbour, an Upper Peninsula native and twenty-five-year resident of Marquette, made an offer on the large, low-rambling building, and, when it was accepted, began renovations.

"My family had been in the restaurant business for some time, owning many Big Boy franchises in the Upper Peninsula," Scott told me. "My dad and I loved to barbeque, and we used to compete against each other and we entered area competitions. We also loved craft beer. But there weren't any barbeque and smoked meat restaurants in the area. The building, the brewing equipment, and the location seemed to be the perfect place to create a family restaurant where people could enjoy good barbeque, and beer made on the premises."

When you enter the brewpub, which opened in 2019, the first impression is of spaciousness. The west side is somewhat dark, with few windows and dark wood paneling. But the east side is bright and airy, looking out on a large beer garden, with a lush lawn and a covered area with picnic tables and space for musicians who regularly perform there.

Although Arbour had home brewed, he hired Grant Lyke, who had worked for many years at Jasper Ridge Brewery in nearby Ishpeming, and who had been the brewer when the place had been Chocolay River Brewery, to start up the brewery. Grant had to begin by draining the beer that had been left in the tanks, and then developed recipes for six craft beers ranging from a light blonde ale to a dark stout. Diners also had other liquor options, including a full bar and a pay-as-you-go, self-serve "tap-table" that offered craft beers from other breweries in the region. Patrons scanned their credit or debit cards, selected the beer they wanted and the number of ounces. They were charged by the ounce.

Lyke also trained Spencer Trubac, who had worked at breweries in the Lower Peninsula and then at the Smokehouse Brewpub as a bartender, on the intricacies of the five-barrel system. When Trubac left to assume the head brewer position at Drifa Brewing, four miles north along the shore, Kyle Peterson, who was working at the bar, took over brewing duties. Kyle, who grew up in Marquette, discovered craft beer while living in North Carolina. "It was Bell's Two Hearted Ale," he remembered, referring to one of Michigan's most popular beers, an IPA named after a river just a hundred miles east of the Upper Peninsula city where he grew up. "I fell in love with IPAs and started craft brewing."

Kyle described the Lake Superior Smokehouse Brewpub beers as the result of an evolving process. Grant Lyke had developed solid recipes of the standard styles and taught them to Scott and Spencer; they tinkered with them, and now Scott and Kyle are doing more tinkering and developing recipes for other styles. "We're a restaurant that makes its own beer, and we're working on our beers to make them equal partners with the food we serve. We want them to be approachable and drinkable and interesting interpretations of older and newer styles," Scott said.

Two beers fit into the crossover category designed to introduce people to craft ales. **Golden Blonde Ale** (ABV 4.7 percent) "is as close to a lager as we've done. We use pilsner and Vienna malts to give a good base, Saaz hops for spiciness, and Willamette hops for peppery and earthy notes." **American Wheat Ale** (ABV 5 percent) is the next step in the entry into the craft beer world. It's a gentle, slightly sweet beer that uses red and white wheat malt and pale malts to create a smooth wheat profile. The Willamette hops, with their earthy and peppery notes, balance the sweetness. The wheat beer is the base for the brewpub's most popular beer, **Blueberry Wheat Ale** (ABV 5.4 percent). "We're not allowed to not have it!" Kyle stated with a chuckle.

If the wheat and the golden blonde ales are fairly conventional craft beers, **Midnight Black Ale** (ABV 5 percent) and **So Long Saison** (ABV 5.5 percent) are somewhat different. Midnight Black, a recipe developed by Grant Lyke and tweaked by Spencer, Scott, and now Kyle, is a slightly-bitter, medium-bodied ale with chocolate and dark coffee notes. Milder than a stout, it is close to a schwarzbier, a German dark beer. So Long Saison is a style that was originally developed in Belgium and was served to farm workers at their midday meal. Low in alcohol, it has peppery notes, along with citrus, floral and piney flavors. It's a smooth, thirst-quenching drink, clean and crisp.

The brewpub's strongest beers are both IPAs. **Hoppy Days IPA** (ABV 6.5 percent) is one of Grant Lyke's recipes, his interpretation of the West Coast Style IPAs that dominated the first two decades of the craft beer movement. "It's, earthy, piney, and grassy. There are four different types of hops used, giving a complex variety of flavors. Even though it has noticeable bitterness, it's not aggressive, in-your-face like some IPAs. It's very popular, even with people who are fairly new to craft beer." **Harvey Haze IPA** (ABV 7.2 percent) is a New England IPA, one of the newer takes on the style that emphasizes a variety of fruit flavors from tropical and citrus to stone fruits. One of the first recipes developed by Scott Arbour, it uses wheat and flaked oats to create a smooth texture and a haziness.

As we finished our conversation, Kyle Peterson reemphasized that although Lake Superior Smokehouse Brewpub was a restaurant that brewed its own beer, he and Scott Arbour were working to make the ales they brewed partners, not just accompaniments to the food. After our conversation, I enjoyed a beef brisket sandwich and the So Long Saison, a perfect pairing for a beer writer on a field trip, and agreed that the two did make good partners.

8 Drifa Brewing Company

Drifa Brewing Company (photo by author)

Address: 501 South Lake St, Marquette, MI 49855
Phone: 906-273-1300
www.drifabrewing.beer
www.facebook.com/drifabrewing

If I'd had both the energy and the time, and if threatening rain clouds hadn't been gathering overhead, I'd have had a snack instead of the very filling and delicious beef brisket sandwich and then walked the block to the North Country Trail and strolled the three miles along the Superior shore to my next destination, Drifa Brewing. Then, my visit there over, I could have walked eight or ten blocks, the last two uphill, to Vierling Restaurant and Marquette Harbor Brewery, and, my appetite increased, enjoyed a full white-fish dinner before conducting my final interview. As it was, I drove north along Highway 28/41 to East Hampton Street, turned left and parked in front of Drifa brewery at 501 South Lake Street.

I'd visited the site five years earlier, shortly after the formation of the Marquette Brewing Coop had been announced. Then there was a virtually empty building, save a long table around which, the previous evening, members of the Marquette Home Brewers club had gathered to taste and discuss fellow members' beers brewed with peppers. I was meeting with David Gill, president of the club, a first-grade teacher, and one of the main organizers of the newly-formed Coop. He was wearing a t-shirt that bore the slogan "Superior Water, Superior Beer," a concept I would hear in various forms many times during my journey. "Inside every home brewer," he told me, "is a secret, or not so secret, desire to become a professional brewer." And that, he explained, was the driving force behind the decision to start a cooperative brewery, one owned, governed and operated by its members.

Before they served their first beer in 2019, the organizers had a great deal to do. In addition the maze of regulations to be navigated in order to get the necessary permits, brewing equipment had to be purchased, the building renovated, and, most important of all, money had to be raised. Already, the brewery had sold one hundred memberships at $99 each and had fulfilled legal requirements to engage in other fundraising projects. Because of a puzzling state regulation, the new brewery could not be called the Marquette Brewing Cooperative. So the name Drifa (pronounced dreefa), a Norwegian word meaning *snow drift*, was chosen—a recognition of the large winter snowfalls of the area and a salute to Scandinavian presence in the area.

On my 2022 visit, I noticed first the beer garden surrounding the building, a wide lawn with picnic tables and large umbrellas and a performance space for the bands that frequently entertain patrons on warm evenings and weekends. Inside was a spacious taproom, a gathering of couches and easy chairs in one corner, a scattering of high tables and stools, and a bar. David Gill, the chairman of the board of the Coop and still an elementary school teacher, was my host, along with recently hired head brewer Spencer Trubac, who until a few weeks ago had held a similar position at Lake Superior Smokehouse Brewpub.

We chatted first about Drifa as a "third place," a term I had learned from a western Canada brewer who described his taproom/restaurant using that term. "It's not home and it's not work; it's a place where people can gather together and feel part of a community." Both Spencer and David agreed with the term. "We see ourselves as part of the South Marquette community; we are kind of the community's gathering place. The regulars get to know each other and us. There are two couples that come in every Tuesday afternoon. They visit with each other and enjoy a couple of beer before going to their homes. People gather for birthday parties and other family events and our regular trivia and open mic nights are very popular with the locals." The taproom and grounds are also made available to charitable groups for their fundraisers.

Spencer Trubac, who grew up in Traverse City in the Lower Peninsula, had crossed the bridge to attend Northern Michigan University in Marquette and then Michigan Tech in Houghton. He had taken courses in pre-med and pre-law before settling on a literature degree. But, perhaps one of his most important learning experiences occurred a few blocks west of the Michigan Tech campus in the Keweenaw Brewing Company taproom: he discovered craft beer. Although he enjoyed his studies in English and American literature, there weren't many jobs in the field and he decided to put his newfound enthusiasm for craft beer to use. Back in Traverse City, he "hung around" the brewers at a couple of brewpubs, learning the ropes of a new field. He returned to Marquette, took a job as a bartender at Lake Superior Smokehouse Brewpub, learning more from brewer Grant Lyke, and then became head brewer. The opportunity to assume a similar role at Drifa, an establishment devoted to brewing beer, came open and he jumped at the opportunity.

As we talked about several of the beer offerings at Drifa, David Gill noted that feedback from patrons, many of whom were members of the Coop and very knowledgeable about craft beer, was very important. Spencer described the overall house style as giving a modern twist to traditional styles and mentioned Drifa's Sustadt, which is a contemporary interpretation of a German alt bier (the name means "old beer") that had been brewed for centuries in Dusseldorf. "I want the beers to be approachable," he continued. "But I give them a little twist to make them distinctive examples of the styles. We don't want to be 'full wild/crazy', but we like being creative."

Drifa offers two beers that could be classified in the crossover category. **Lower Harbor American Lager** (ABV 5.1 percent) is a style that most brewers eschewed in the early days of the craft brewing movement. Now many are offering a lager that is similar to the most popular brands of the large, international brewers. Brewed with flaked corn (which gives a bready texture and flavor) and

Vienna malts, which impart a nutty and honey flavor, it is balanced by the Sterling hops, which add spiciness. Overall, it possesses a fuller body and more complex array of flavors than mainstream lagers, while at the same time being very approachable for newcomers to craft beer. **Pigeon Feathers Cream Ale** (ABV 5 percent), which has a smooth, bready texture, but also some hop spiciness, is a fuller-bodied beer than Lower Park.

Sustadt Alt (ABV 6.5 percent) and **Walk of Shame Brown Ale** (ABV 5.3 percent) are two of the brewery's most popular darker ales. Sustadt (the name means south side of town in German), one of only a couple of examples of alt beer I've found in the UP, is an amber-colored ale with a bready malt flavor, along with caramel and toasted notes and a crisp hop finish. Walk of Shame is a rich, full-bodied dark beer made from a variety of ingredients: crystal dark malts give burnt caramel, toffee, and raisin flavors; chocolate wheat malts add cocoa notes; Columbus and Cascade hops contribute earthy, pepper, and grapefruit flavors. A pound of whole bean coffee and a gallon and a half of cold brew coffee are added to each two barrel batch.

Drifa has created interpretations of both West Coast and East Coast IPAs. **Green Ladder IPA** (6.8) the West Coast offering, features Maris Otter malts, noted for a nutty, biscuity and sweet flavor that is balanced by the Columbus, Citra, and Mosaic hops that add citrus, floral, peppery, piney and bubble gum flavors. **Judy's Big Booty** (ABV 6.5 percent), which is named after Trubac's automobile, is a New England IPA and is fuller-bodied, sweeter, and less bitter than Green Ladder. Simcoe hops give the grapefruit "juiciness" characteristic of the style, while wheat malt creates the haziness and oat malts the fuller body.

⑨ Marquette Harbor Brewery at Vierling Restaurant

Marquette Harbor Brewery (photo by author)

Address: 119 Front Street, Marquette, MI 49855
Phone: 906-228-333,
www.facebook.com/TheVierling

When we'd finished our discussions at Lake Superior Smokehouse Brewpub, the threatening clouds had passed by without any rain, and several people jogging along the North Country Trail dropped in to quench their thirsts. Thanking my hosts for their generous gift of samples to take home, I departed and drove the last half mile to my final stop of the day: the Vierling Restaurant and Marquette Harbor Brewery. But first I made a quick detour across Highway 41 to Division Street to look at an 1850s building that had been purchased by a group intending to convert the structure into a brewery. Plans for a 2020 opening had been announced, but when I walked around the locked building and looked in the windows in 2022, there was no evidence of any renovation or new construction. Perhaps the anonymous purchasers had decided that with ten breweries already operating in Marquette County and another scheduled to open in the fall of 2022, the area had enough for the present.

The final stop on the shoreline ale trail was the county's pioneer craft brewery: the Marquette Harbor Brewery at the Vierling Restaurant. I'd been visiting the restaurant with friends and family for over three-and-a-half decades and, in the summer of 1996, a year after the brewery opened, I had enjoyed my first glass of Upper Peninsula craft beer there.

From the outside, the space it occupies at the corner of Front and Main Streets looks very ordinary. With the appropriate signage, it could be an old-fashioned corner grocery store or secondhand emporium. But when you open the screen door and enter, it's like stepping back over 125 years and entering a very classy bar and saloon. That's exactly what Terry and Kristi Doyle wanted to recreate when, in 1983, they bought part of a building that had recently been a bakery/coffee shop. They wanted to make the interior resemble what it was in 1918, when, a year after the establishment of prohibition in Michigan the Vierling Saloon closed its doors after thirty-five years of operation.

They certainly succeeded. To the left of the entrance is an antique oak bar and behind its serving area a full-length wall mirror reflecting the many colored bottles of liquor and liqueur standing in front of it. Lining the original brick walls are nineteenth-century paintings, some of them from the collection of Louis Vierling, the original saloon owner, along with old photographs of buildings and street scenes from Marquette of well over a century ago. The windows at the back of the restaurant incorporate some of the original stained glass and look out onto the (now decommissioned) Lower Harbor Ore Dock, which stands eighty-five feet high and extends nearly a thousand feet from the shore.

I first met Terry Doyle in 2011, at which time we talked about the history of his restaurant/brewpub. "We wanted to have a restaurant close to downtown that would appeal to the local business crowd along with tourists. One of the things we wanted was good imported beer to complement our menu, and so we stocked Bass Pale Ale, Guinness Stout, and Heineken Lager. Right from the beginning our patrons had good beer to drink."

In 1992, a Michigan State Law was passed that permitted restaurants to brew and sell beer on their premises. "The merchants were anxious to have a brewpub in downtown Marquette in order

to draw more shoppers away from the outlying malls. And I
thought, 'Why not us?' We opened the brewery in 1995. We knew
we had to have good beer and to do that, we needed a brewer who
could create a quality product." Doyle had to look no further than
the restaurant's kitchen to find the right person. Derek "Chumley"
Anderson (the nickname was given him by his older brother's high
school buddies) had worked in the kitchen since the restaurant's
earliest days and had risen to the position of senior cook. "We call
him the 'scholarly brewer'," Terry remarked. "He's always
studying; he reads and rereads all the books about brewing, and he
keeps very careful notes about the different beers he's created."

When I interviewed Chumley later that day, he remembered. "I
was ready for a change when Terry approached me. Running a
small brewery seemed like a good idea. I had no brewery training; I
learned on the job." The person who had been sent to set up the
five barrel brewing system came with three recipes, walked Chumley
through them, and then left. "I took copious notes, which I still
have. I began reading books and talked with John Malchow, the
original brewer at Hereford & Hops in Escanaba."

Chumley invited me to look over the brewery that was a few feet
below the table where we were sitting. If walking into the restaurant
had been like going back to the late nineteenth century, walking
down the steep and narrow stairs into the basement was almost like
entering a medieval dungeon. Thick walls of cut stone and mortar
had provided the foundation for the building since it had been built
well over 140 years ago. Very little light reflected off of them.
However, as we turned the corner of the shadowy corridor at the
bottom of the stairs, we entered a bright and airy brewhouse. Light
shone in from large windows on the southern and eastern sides of
the building, making the freshly-polished tanks glisten. Looking out
the windows, you could see the sun glinting off the waters in the
harbor.

Chumley sat on the platform where the mash tun and brew kettle
stood, and I sat on a folding chair below as we talked about the
beers Marquette Harbor Brewing produced and how these related
to the restaurant just above our heads. "We're a restaurant that
makes its own beer," he explained. "Beer accounts for only about
15 percent of our business, food most of the rest." As a result, he
brews what he called "standard American ales—clean and well-
balanced. I don't get too far out of the box and aim for consistency

from brew to brew." He noted that he created beer for a wide range of people: business men and women, university professors, legal-aged university students, and tourists, many of them beer tourists.

When I visited him five years later, after I'd been at Drifa Brewing, we sat in the same area: he on the platform, me on a folding chair. When I asked him what had changed, he noted all the rapid changes in the craft brewing industry: the increasing varieties of pale ales, the growing popularity of sour beers, and the reintroduction of lagers. But when he showed me the current beer menu, it was very similar to the one I'd seen on my earlier visit. In fact, two of his earliest brews, Honey Wheat and Pale Ale were still on the list, along with Blueberry Wheat, which was introduced a few months after the restaurant began producing its own beers. "We've done a little tinkering and we've tried some of the new hop varietals that have come out; but there haven't been any radical changes."

As it has been for many years, **Blueberry Wheat** (ABV 5.3 percent) is Chumley's most popular creation. "I'd helped Lark Ludlow at Tahquamenon Falls Brewery create a blueberry ale for a festival in Paradise, Michigan, and, then, using the wheat recipe that came with our equipment, made one for Marquette's Blueberry Festival. We brew it all year around now. We use our honey wheat ale as the base and add pure blueberry extract." Light-bodied, the wheat beer has a crispness created by the use of Saaz hops. The blueberry flavor does not overwhelm, a danger in making fruit beers, but is a nice complement to the wheat malt base and clover honey.

Other regulars include **Blonde Ale** (ABV 4.9 percent), a light-bodied, slightly malty beer designed as an entry level ale that is given a slight spiciness by the Hallertau hops. **Red Ale** (ABV 5.4 percent) is sweeter and maltier than the Blonde Ale, while the **Stout** (ABV 4.5 percent) is dryer and sweeter than the well-known Guinness. **Pale Ale** (ABV 6.7 percent) is listed on the menu as an American Pale Ale, but "It's really more an IPA," Chumley confessed. He uses Cascade and Centennial hops, which add grape-fruit flavors and bitterness, respectively. There are two regular IPA offerings: **Laid Back IPA** (ABV 5 percent), a session IPA that has a caramel sweetness that is balanced by the hops, and **Chum's Double Pale Ale** (ABV 8.5 percent), which is very hop-forward and, as the menu notes, "not for the light beer drinker."

   Chumley came across during our visit as a relatively soft-spoken, laid-back person. But during both of the conversations I've had with him, I'd noticed a spark in his eyes and enthusiasm in his voice. "You've got to have a passion if you want to brew. You have to be able to create. I couldn't be a corporate brewer [his term for employees of the enormous multinational breweries]. I'd never last." After over a quarter of a century, the UP's longest-serving brewer still had the passion, as strong as ever.

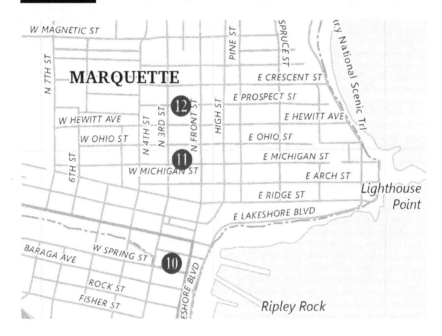

After 1868, when downtown Marquette was destroyed by fire, all new buildings had to be constructed of brick or sandstone. A century later, a calamity of another kind hit the downtown area. As the population grew, many businesses moved out from the center of town. In 1971, Marquette Mall opened along Michigan Highway 28 west and, a decade later, Westwood Mall opened a mile or so further out. The center of town was suffering. But around this time, a revitalization of the downtown started to take place. In 1976, the Savings Bank at the corner of Front and Washington, which had been built in 1892, was completely renovated. In 1986, Terry and Kristi Doyle opened the Vierling Restaurant in a building that had been a saloon in the 1890s. As the twentieth century moved to a close, old homes and small commercial buildings were being restored and turned into locally owned shops and restaurants along Third Street, which extends from downtown north toward the edges of Northern Michigan University. Vibrancy was returning to the inner city and surrounding areas.

Craft breweries played a part in the restoration and rejuvenation. Marquette Harbor Brewery, which opened in 1995 in the Vierling Restaurant, was the first brewery in the city after Upper Peninsula Brewing closed in 1919. Since 2010, there has been an explosion of breweries in the downtown/Third Street area: Blackrocks in 2010, Ore Dock in 2012, and Superior Culture in 2017. Kognisjon Brygerri is scheduled to open in Spring 2023. By 2023 it will be possible to enjoy a leisurely fourteen-block pub crawl from Ore Dock to Kognisjon Brygerri. You can bring your own snacks or take-out food and sit outside on warm days, or, if it's not so warm, sit inside and enjoy the local beer and entertainment. As I made the stroll on a June afternoon, I nicknamed the route, the "ale trail of the three Rs," as the breweries were housed in buildings that had been reclaimed, restored, and repurposed.

⑩ Ore Dock Brewing Company

Ore Dock Brewing Company (photo by author)

Address: 114 Spring St, Marquette, MI 49855
Phone: 906-228-8888
www.oredockbrewing.com
www.facebook.com/OreDock

Located a block-and-a-half away from the giant structure that gives it its name, Ore Dock Brewing Company was opened in 2012 by Andrea and Wes Persteiner. Having visited brewpubs across the country, they were impressed at these places where people could gather, where "craft beer and community meet." When I first visited Ore Dock in 2017, I noticed that the front windows were covered with posters announcing upcoming events: live music, a science panel, a drama, and a fifth anniversary celebration of Ore Dock's founding.

The Pernsteiners found a downtown building that was big enough to house a brewery along with space for all the activities and events they wanted to hold, a later nineteenth-century structure that most recently had been the home of an automobile dealership. "There were thirty cars on the second floor when we acquired the building," Andrea remembered. "Luckily there was a ramp so that we could get them down and out. When we began renovations, we tried as much as possible to keep the character of the place. It's such an important part of Marquette's history."

Andrea gave me a tour, pointing out the changes. The first floor was the least interesting, looking just like what it was: a friendly neighborhood taproom. At the front was a large roll-up door that opened to a sidewalk seating area from which, if you sat in just the right place, you could see the ore dock. After we had looked down toward the water, she led me upstairs to what Nick VanCourt, the founding brewer, had called "Marquette's living room."

"We named our IPA 'Reclamation' in part to symbolize what we have done to the building, especially on this floor." There's a large bar, the top of which is decorated with iron ore pellets scavenged from beside the railroad tracks leading to the still operating Upper Harbor Ore Dock, a stage where local and touring musicians perform, a fireplace, and, at the front, comfortable chairs and sofas. "In our renovations, we used recognizable Upper Peninsula design elements: wood, brick, concrete and steel. And we hired many local people to do the work. It's a big room with a lot of different areas. On weekday afternoons, we call it 'Study Hall.' High school and university students can come up here and work on group projects or simply read or write. Other people will come up and have a meeting." Individuals often saunter about looking at the local art that is hung on the walls.

We sat in one of the easy chairs and talked about the beers. I began by asking her why, in a relatively small city, she and Wes had decided to open a third brewery. (Blackrocks had begun operations a year-and-a-half earlier; the Vierling Restaurant had been serving their own beer for over a decade-and-a-half.) She noted that each place was different. "We had a different vision—we weren't going to be a restaurant or just a taproom; we wanted a community space for everyone, people of different ages and backgrounds. That was one of the things we liked in Europe when we visited German beer gardens."

Talking of the beers, she explained: "We wanted to take traditional styles and reintroduce them to people. It was a kind of reclamation project." The Pernsteiners knew that to do that they'd need a professional brewer, one with the experience not just to create these styles, but to make them consistent from batch to batch and consistently good. They found their brewer in Nick VanCourt, who had studied brewing at Chicago's prestigious Siebel Institute, had several years of brewing experience in Wisconsin, and who had become a partner as well as head brewer. When, after four years, he left to start his own brewery, Barrel + Beam, he was replaced by Jake Shea. A native of Alpena in the Lower Peninsula, Shea had studied microbiology at Northern Michigan University. He was a home brewer and, when he learned about Ore Dock, he applied to become VanCourt's assistant.

When I revisited Ore Dock in June 2022, Shea was still the head brewer while VanCourt's Barrel + Beam was thriving on the west side of town. Andea Persteiner and I again sat in the second floor "living room." When I asked her about changes that had taken place she took me to the back door, opened it, and gestured to the land below the steps and to a nearly derelict building beside it. The area was to be the site of a reclamation project: the building was to be torn down, a beer garden created where people could sit on warm spring and summer days, sip beer, and listen to music. We returned to the second floor "living room," where we discussed changes within the brewery. She noted that she, the brew crew, and the staff had listened carefully to their customers, who had become more knowledgeable beer drinkers. "They enjoy taking risks, trying new and different beers. We were very focused on Belgian style beers at first, but we have ranged beyond them." Reclamation IPA, Porter, Bum's Beach Wheat Ale, and Blond, which I had tasted five years ago, were still around, but there were a lot of new creations.

Andrea discussed her "six pack of beers," an interesting mix of old and new, all of which are, as one of the Ore Dock slogans proclaims, "What water wants to be." She began with **Reclamation IPA** (ABV 7 percent), the brewery's flagship beer, on the can of which was an illustration of the State Bank building that had been "reclaimed" in the 1970s. She referred to it as a mid-coast IPA, not as hoppy as varieties from the West Coast, nor as hazy as those from the East Coast. Munich, Carapils, and caramel malts provide a grainy, nutty, caramel-flavored base against which are played the citrusy, floral, spicy, and piney notes of the Cascade, Chinook, and Columbus hops. It's a rounded, balanced ale that uses Michigan hops as much as possible. The simply named**Porter** (ABV 5.6 percent), another standby, uses Munich, caramel, amber, black, and chocolate malts to create a complex coffee and bitter-sweet chocolate taste, while the Fuggle hops contribute an earthiness.

Andrea's next two choices represented Ore Dock's contribution to the growing popularity in the UP of fruit flavored beers. The first **Blue Canoe** (ABV 4.3 percent), is a different approach to the seemingly "mandatory" requirement that a UP brewery have available what some people have called the UP's "National Beer,"a blueberry ale. It's a wheat beer, as many of them are, but a different kind of wheat beer: a Berliner Weisse, one of the mildest, gentlest of sour beers. "We didn't want fruit beers at first, but we listened," Andrea explained. It is tart, but light-bodied, with a "hint" of blueberries—a refreshing summer beer. The other, **Bramble on Rose Belgian Strong Ale** (ABV 8.3 percent), combines the sweet-tartness of raspberries, a spicy hint of rosehips, and a bubblegum flavor that is contributed by the yeast. It goes down easily, but be careful!

The final two choices were a light-bodied kolsch, a German beer that has sometimes been called the ale that wants to be a lager, and a dunkel, another German style, dark in color and fuller in body. **Queen City Kolsch** (ABV 4.7 percent) is a wonderfully crisp, refreshing beer that can serve as a crossover for craft beer newbies. The Hallertau Mittelfruh hops provide a spiciness balanced by the slight sweetness of the pilsner and caramel malts. **Six Pointer Munich Dunkel** (ABV 5.7 percent) is dominated by the Munich, Victory, and black malts, which give a rich, nutty, and roasted flavor balanced by the fruity, spicy flavors of the Hallertau hops. The beer is named after a six-pointed hat popular among Yoopers during the hunting season.

When I left Ore Dock carrying a six pack of the different beers we discussed, it was a warm, sunshiny June afternoon. But, for a moment, I felt a tinge of regret; I almost wished it were late April and that I were at one of Marquette's really fun end-of-winter celebrations: the Festival of the Angry Bear. The Ore Dock Building, along with Spring Street, is the site of displays, food booths, music, crowning of a festival queen, and the coming out of hibernation of a barrel-paged European-style beer: "Angry Bear." But it wasn't April, so I would have to content myself with going back to the cabin and sitting on the dock of the bay doing research—making tasting notes on the Ore Dock beers I was sipping.

⑪ Blackrocks Brewery

Blackrocks Brewery (photo by author)

Address: 424 North Third St, Marquette, MI 49855
Phone: 906-273-1333
www.blackrocksbrewery.com,
www.facebook.com/BlackrocksBrewery

The story of Blackrocks Brewery, the second stop on the "Three Rs trail," involves another "living room,"—a real one. Toward the end of the first decade of this century, Andy Langlois and David Manson, two home-brewing friends, found themselves unemployed when the pharmaceutical companies they worked for as sales reps downsized. "We decided to stay in Marquette," Andy told me when I first met him in 2011, a few months after Blackrocks had opened, "and turn our home brewing hobby into a profession and start a brewery." They bought an old house in the Third Street village area, transformed it into a brewery and taproom, and hired Andrew Reeves, who had worked for New Holland Brewing in the Lower Peninsula and from whom they had bought home brew supplies at the nearby Whites Party Store, as head brewer.

Marquette's second craft brewery was an instant success. "We opened just after Christmas in 2010, and we ran out of beer!" Andy Langlois recalled as we sat in what used to be the living room of the building that has since been nicknamed "The Little Yellow House on the Corner [of North Third and West Michigan]." This happened so often that one of the employees jokingly suggested that they list their opening hours as 5:00 pm "until we run out."

They began brewing with a one-barrel system, which was fitted snugly into what must, at one time, have been the kitchen. "We've done over fifty different beers since we started," he told me at that time. "We don't have a standard house list. Wide variety is our strength. We like to brew what's fun for us. We'd be bored with a limited list." In other words, if you'd visited once a week, there'd be a different offering of beers listed on the chalkboard by the front door. Some of them had some interesting and unusual ingredients. One of the stouts used chipotle as an additive, while another ale, a porter, included mint.

The living room (i.e., the taproom) only seated thirty people at first and was very frequently filled to capacity. Some people came by bike, others walked. There were people from the neighborhood, Northern Michigan University (just a half mile north of "The "Little Yellow House"), businessmen from downtown, doctors and nurses from the hospital, and, as the weather warmed up, tourists. Blackrocks didn't (and still doesn't) serve food, but patrons often bring takeout from nearby restaurants or have food delivered. "One time, a family came, spread out a tablecloth and napkins, dishes and cutlery, and served a picnic lunch they'd brought from home." Andy remarked that sometimes being in the taproom seemed like being at an extended family gathering or neighborhood get-together.

When, in 2017, I met again with Andy, David, and Andrew, there had been a lot of changes at Blackrocks. "The Little Yellow House on the Corner" had been renovated again: the taproom had been extended to the second floor and the backyard parking lot was now a patio. The one-barrel brewhouse was still churning out beer after beer, but to keep up with the demand, a three-barrel system had been added. The most significant change took place in 2013. Andy Langlois and David Manson had decided to upgrade Blackrocks into a production brewery and turned a building that had once been a soft drink bottling plant into a twenty-barrel brewhouse. Chris Hutte, one of Andrew Reeves' home brewing friends and assistant, took over brewing at "The Little House," making limited editions, test brews, and one-offs. Andrew was in charge of brewing operations at the new production facility. Here he developed a line of year-around, seasonal, and specialty brews that were distributed in the Upper and then Lower Peninsula, and later northern Wisconsin. The second craft beer production facility in the Upper Peninsula (in 2004,Keweenaw Brewing in Houghton became the first) made its product available in cans right from the start. In 2014, production was 4,500 barrels; by 2017, it had risen to 6,500.

By the summer of 2022, more changes had taken place. In the previous year, the number of barrels brewed had passed the ten thousand mark for the first time, making Blackrocks one of three UP breweries (the other two were Keweenaw and Upper Hand) to reach five figures in production. And "The "Little Yellow House" had expanded. In 2019, the owners purchased the building next door, formerly the home of a small business and two apartments. The pandemic slowed down the process of renovations, which included a retail space, a taproom, a second-story deck overlooking the street, and an inside balcony overlooking the lower part of the taproom. There was also an outdoor fireplace and a smaller one inside. An indoor hallway joined the "old" and "new" taprooms.

Andy Langlois proudly showed me through the expanded facilities on a sunny June afternoon. It wasn't happy hour time yet, but already several patrons were relaxing in the indoor and outdoor seating areas, enjoying the beers that Chris Hutte had created specially for the taproom. These included **Cockney Mild** (ABV 4.0 percent), a dark, malty English Dark Mild, a lower-alcohol favorite in British pubs, and **Table Bier**, another lower alcohol beer (ABV 3.9 percent) based on a Belgian ale traditionally served at lunch to thirsty farm workers.

I asked Andy if, when he and David Manson purchased "The Little Yellow House on the Corner," he had ever expected it to grow to this size or to see Blackrocks' beers available throughout Michigan and in parts of Wisconsin. "No, we never believed it would be this successful. We started simply on a small system, producing batch after batch, learning about the different styles and variations and introducing these to the people around town. We wanted this to be a place that people came for a pint of beer made where they were drinking it—there wasn't anything like that at a time. We expanded slowly, reinvesting the money we made back into the business. Now we can get three hundred people in here. But it's still a part of this wonderful, funky neighborhood."

Later that afternoon, I dropped in at the production brewery to chat with Andrew Reeves and fellow-brewer Charles Hotelling. Andrew described the house style as "simple, agreeable, approachable," adding: "We want to create beers that people will enjoy drinking. Beer is an affordable luxury; it's for everyone." He went on to say that while they are not trend-driven, they do like to brew both the kinds of hoppy beers that have dominated beer lists since the earlier decades of the craft movement, and lagers, which have become more and more popular in recent years as people have come to realize that this style of beer doesn't have to taste like the bland products of the international giants.

Not surprisingly, the six-pack (plus two) that Andrew and Charles chose to describe included IPAs and Lagers. **51K American IPA** (ABV 7 percent) is named after the distance of a local ski race plus the one kilometer distance from its finish to the Blackrocks' taproom. The brewery's top-seller, it was described by the brewers as resinous, dank, and very aromatic. Columbus, Comet, and Nugget hops provide spicy, citrusy, and herbal qualities that are balanced by the slightly caramel and bready notes of the Vienna and wheat malts. **MyKiss IPA** (ABV 7.5 percent), a companion IPA, is "juicier" with the Citra, Simcoe, Mosaic hops providing a variety of fruit flavors, along with piney and earthy notes.

The three lagers Andrew and Charles talked about (there is also a Mexican lager periodically available in the tap room) are released seasonally. **Classic Pilsner** (ABV 5.5 percent) is available from October through February. A German version of the style, it has a spicy, citrusy taste created by the German Magnum and Tettnang hops, and a bready, nutty quality from the pilsner malts. Somewhat sweeter and maltier than Czech pilsners, it has "everything German in it except the water. Lake Superior water is really good for making Pilsner." **Super Deluxe Helles** (ABV 4.8 percent) is available from May to July and is a softer and maltier beer than the Pilsner. It has less hop zing. **Oktoberfest** (ABV 5.8 percent) is the fall offering (September to November). Honey-amber in color, it is a malt-rich beer, with Munich and Vienna malts giving a strong base. The hops provide a dry, clean finish.

The best word to characterize the last three included in the "six-pack plus two" is "interesting." Each is a seasonal offering. **Honey Lav** (ABV 5.2 percent) is an American wheat ale that includes honey malt, Michigan honey, and whole flowers of English lavender. It is slightly sweet, but not overwhelming, and the lavender adds an understated herbal flavor. It's the beer I must have in the fridge when my daughter comes to visit the Upper Peninsula. **Coconut Brown Ale** (ABV 6 percent) is a unique twist on what has long been a standard beer in English pubs. It's a little hoppier, and, it has coconut flavor. Andrew Reeves is known for having fun experimenting with different ingredients and has added just enough coconut flakes to evoke Hawaii without making the ale taste like suntan lotion. It's available from October to March. **Barbaric Yawp Scotch Ale** is, at 11 percent ABV, Blackrock's heftiest beer. Made from a variety of malts, it is aged for over a year in rum and bourbon oak barrels and emerges as a rich, full-bodied brew with caramel, dried fruit, and smoky flavors.

A few weeks later, as I was checking my notes against the descriptions on the brewery's website, I noticed something very different and funny. After the description of each beer was a suggested food pairing. There have been many books and articles suggesting how well various styles of beer go with specific, often epicurean, foods, sort of like wine. Tongue-in-cheek, the notes suggested such foods as fish sticks, soft pretzels, a drippy ice-cream cone, roasted meat with cigarettes, and grilled spam. When it came time to sit on the dock testing the Blackrocks beers, I didn't have any of these foods and I have never smoked cigarettes. So I sat and enjoyed the lagers and ales for what they are: very good and very flavorful beers.

⑫ Superior Culture

Superior Culture (photo by author)

Address: 717 North Third St, Marquette, MI 49855
Phone: 906-273-0927
www.superiorculturemqt.com,
www.facebook.com/superiorculturemqt

On the other side of Third Street and two and a half blocks north from Blackrocks is another late nineteenth-century building that had once been someone's home and has recently been repurposed. Since 2018, it has been the home of Superior Culture. In the early afternoon of a warm day in June, I mounted the steps at 717 Third Street, paused briefly on the front veranda in the shade created by hop bines climbing upward from the railing, and then entered what had been a family's living room many decades ago. It was now Superior Culture's taproom, somewhat smaller than the original one at Blackrocks had been. There was a small bar, three or four tables, a little performance area, and a lounge with a couple of easy chairs and a couch.

Perhaps the most surprising aspect of the taproom was the ceiling. Covering materials had been torn off, exposing bare beams. I was wondering what was happening when Alex Rowland, the owner and chief brewer, entered. He'd been at the Downtown

Marquette Farmers Market several blocks south on Third, where he sold the brewery's products. He'd noticed me looking up when he'd come in and explained what was going on. He'd done some renovations when he'd taken over the building, creating brewing and taproom space while living upstairs. Now he was doing reclamation work, stripping the building to its original bare bones and restoring it to the way it was so long ago.

He had first visited the Upper Peninsula while he was a student at Michigan State University studying Biological Systems Engineering, a program designed, according to the university's website, to train graduates to work in professions that, among other things, assist in the production of safe food and healthy ecosystems. After his 2014 graduation, he moved north of the bridge to Marquette where his home brewing hobby grew into a business in which he produced kombucha, a fermented tea, along with mead, cider, and beer, which he sold at, among other places, farmers markets and festivals, and, since 2018, at the taproom/brewery.

At the time of my visit, there were no beers available, but Alex talked about his philosophy of brewing and about a few of the beers he had made. He began by noting that, with a one-barrel brewing system, he was able to experiment freely and to rotate a variety of beer styles. "I think the thing is to begin simple—have a blank template for painting an array of flavors. I try to source locally as many of my ingredients as possible." Often he uses a simple malt base to create simple ales to serve as the base for his creations. Of course, Superior Culture used Superior water. Then there are the hops growing on the veranda. When grain was being malted at Upper Peninsula Malting in nearby K. I. Sawyer, he used it and, when Emily Geiger, then of Finlandia University, was culturing local yeasts, he drew from her supply. He's a regular shopper at the local farmers market, where he keeps his eye open for fruits, vegetables, herbs and spices he might use for new creations. "I can hardly wait for the raspberries to arrive each year," he tells me. And, he's a forager. "I could become a professional forager," he confesses with a chuckle. In the nearby forests and fields, he harvests spruce tips and birch bark, each in the proper season.

His descriptions of the ales reveal his philosophy in action. **Birch Beer** (ABV 5.5 percent) begins with the spring harvesting of the inner bark of birches, which is boiled down to make a syrup; he also adds mushrooms and fungi that have medicinal benefits. **UP**

Maple Beer (ABV 5 percent) is a porter using products harvested and boiled down by a friend who has a sugar shack. **Choco Cherry Brown Ale** (4.6 ABV) uses eagerly awaited cherries from the Traverse City area; while **Honey Booch Pale Ale**(4.0) starts with a pale ale base that is infused with kombucha, a fermented tea beverage, and then flavored with lemon, basil, and local honey. And **Front Porch Session IPA** (ABV n/a) uses hops harvested on the veranda.

Alex invited me to come back the next time he had a couple of his ales on tap and I happily accepted. I then crossed back to the east side of Third Street and strolled another three blocks north to my final stop on this ale trail. My destination wasn't a brewery—yet. It was the former home of Valle's Supermarket, a place that during the last couple of years was being transformed into Third Street Marketplace, a gathering of eateries, a comic book and game store, and a brewery: Kognisjon Bryggeri (a Norwegian name for what would become a companion brewery to Ishpeming's Cognition Brewery). A developer who had purchased the building and decided to divide the space into a number of small businesses approached Jay Clancey, the owner of Cognition, about opening a brewery there. "It was a good idea," Clancey remembered. "There was a lot of foot traffic along Third and it was close to both downtown and the university. There will be lots of room and there are plenty of nearby places to buy food. Even now, there are food trucks in the parking lot." Although the pandemic had slowed progress, Clancey planned to open during Spring 2023. The Norwegian name, which would distinguish it from the Ishpeming operation, was chosen for legal reasons. The brew crew at Cognition would also brew at the new location on seven and 3.5-barrel systems, and the beers would be similar to those at Cognition. There were tentative plans to can product for distribution in the Upper Peninsula.

I passed the two food trucks in the parking lot and peered through a window on which was taped a building permit for the new brewery. At the far end of a large, quite empty space, I could see the brewing tanks. I wouldn't be around in the winter when Kognisjon was up and running, but I looked forward to a late spring visit next year, when I would travel the ale trail along Third, stopping at buildings that had been reclaimed, restored or renovated, and repurposed, and all of them offering great Upper Peninsula beer.

Marquette (west), Negaunee, Ishpeming

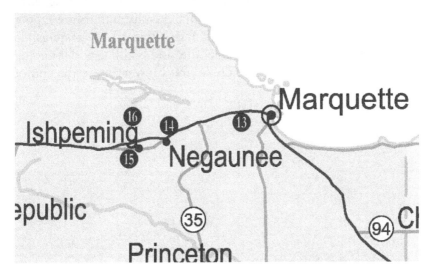

In 1844, William Burt, the head of the surveying party mapping the Upper Peninsula, made an amazing discovery: an enormous deposit of iron ore near Negaunee. Within a few years, the area had become the site the growing nation's latest boom: mines sprung up around Negaunee and Ishpeming, which became the most important towns in the northern central Upper Peninsula. Marquette, by contrast, was significant mainly as the location of docks where iron ore mined in the western part of the county was loaded onto freighters. Until 1920, Ishpeming was the Marquette County's largest city, reaching a population high of over thirteen thousand in 1910, while Marquette had a population of eighty-four hundred. However, as the mining industry declined in the twentieth century, the populations of Negaunee and Ishpeming dropped steadily. In 2020, the former had a population of 4,627 and the latter, 6,140.

The western half of Marquette County has seen a revival during the first two decades of the twenty-first century. Big box stores now line Highway 28 on the way out of Marquette and new subdivisions are being built. Both Negaunee and Ishpeming are working on restoring historic buildings in their downtown areas. The craft beer movement has been part of this rejuvenation. In 1996, Jasper Ridge Brewery opened in a shopping complex next to Highway 28 north of Ishpeming. Cognition Brewery opened in 1915 in a historic building in the city's downtown. Three years later, Barrel + Beam opened in the outskirts of Marquette in a building that had once been home to one of the most popular restaurants in the Upper Peninsula. And, in 2022, two Negaunee citizens were responsible for restoring a more than twelve-decades-old building and founding Upper Peninsula Brewing, the city's first brewery since the end of the nineteenth century.

⑬ Barrel + Beam Brewing Company

Barrel + Beam Brewing Company

Address: 260 Northwoods Rd, Marquette, MI 49855
Phone: 906-273-2559,
www.barrelandbeam.com
www.facebook.com/barrelandbeam

I first visited the future home of Barrel + Beam in the summer of 2017. "You go past Walmart heading west on 28, turn left at Harbor Freight and go past Menards until you reach the old Northwoods Supper Club building. You'll see lots of construction trucks and tradesmen's vehicles; we've been renovating since May. One of our first jobs was removing a bunch of squatters: a family of raccoons," co-owner and head brewer Nick VanCourt told me. When I turned in, he was finishing a conversation with a group of people holding blueprints. He welcomed me and took me on a tour of the building. "Here is where our brewhouse will be; these are the foeders [large wooden barrels used to ferment and age beer]; our taproom will be over here and outside we'll have a biergarten.

"What is that?" I asked, pointing to a shallow, rectangular trough mounted on wheels.

"That's a coolship," Nick replied. "We fill it with wort [unfermented beer] and wheel it to where it will be exposed to wild yeast floating in the air. It's called natural fermentation."

The tour over, we moved to a quiet area away from the sounds of the renovations going on. I sat on an old chair, Nick, on a four legged-bathtub that had come with the building and for some reason was in the middle of the room. I asked Nick if, in addition to beer, he was thinking of making bathtub gin. He said no, but that there would be cider and mead.

Nick and his wife, Marina Dupler, who is co-owner of Barrel + Beam, grew up in the south central UP town of Daggett. It was while he was working at the Great Dane Brewpub in Madison, Wisconsin, that he became interested in what would become his passion: brewing beer, especially Belgian styles of beer. He began his professional training at the prestigious Siebel Institute of Technology in Chicago and then spent a year at the Doemens Academy in Munich. During his time in Europe, he made a trip to Belgium, where he "really discovered Belgian beer styles." Back in Wisconsin, he worked at Tyranena Brewing, where he had a chance to try out his new knowledge.

While in Wisconsin, he became acquainted with Andrea and Wes Pernsteiner, who were in the planning stages of opening Ore Dock Brewing in Marquette. He asked if he could join them as a brewer and returned to the Upper Peninsula as head brewer and part-owner of the new venture. "Wes and Andrea gave me great freedom in the brewhouse. I created a range of beers to appeal to the diversity of people who visited our taproom. The styles included IPAs and Belgian saisons." A glance at the beer lists from Ore Dock's first four years reveals both the standard range of such craft beers as IPAs, Amber Ales, Stouts and Porters, along with several that were labeled saisons or farmhouse beers, the ales that centuries ago had been brewed to quench the thirsts of hard-working agricultural laborers in Belgium.

I asked Nick, why, with a brewpub and two breweries with taprooms in Marquette, another three in the county, and at least one more on the drawing board, he and his wife had decided to start their own brewery. His first answer was one I'd heard many times: ever since his home brewing days, he'd dreamt of having his own brewery. But, he went on to offer a more complex reason. While working at Ore Dock, he became more and more focused on producing farmhouse ales, barrel-aged beers, and other funky styles like the ones he'd discovered on his vacation in Belgium. He'd build his brewery with a taproom, but he'd also make it a production facility, one that supplied his specialty beers to other places in the Upper Peninsula and beyond. In 2016, he purchased the eighty-year-old Northwoods Supper Club building, which had been vacant for a decade, began extensive renovations in the spring of 2017, and installed his brewhouse. Barrel + Beam, named after the fermenting and aging vessels in the brewery and the ceiling beams in the restored building, opened for business in 2018.

I visited Nick again in 2022. The raccoons were long gone, the bathtub had disappeared, and the building had been restored to its original 1930s glory. The place had become a popular event center for weddings and other celebratory events. Plans were underway to offer a small food menu, such items as specialty sandwiches and charcuterie boards. Barrel + Beam's beers were available in Michigan and Wisconsin. "We're a niche brewery," Nick remarked. "Because the local area itself isn't large enough to support the styles we have available, distribution is important."

Asked to describe the general house style of his beers, VanCourt explained that they could be classified as "Old World Meets New"—ages-old traditional styles created with modern equipment and featuring, as much as possible, Michigan ingredients. A recent list of Barrel + Beam beers includes such relatively unknown styles as lambic, saison, wit bier, sour ale, wild ale, biere de coupage, grisette, kellerbier, and sahti. The water, of course, is from nearby Lake Superior; some of the yeasts are floating around in the woods beside the brewery; many of the malts come from Great Lakes Malting in Traverse City; local hops are used whenever possible; local fruits, vegetables, and spices, including foraged juniper boughs, contribute to the various brews' distinctive flavors.

The first two beers Nick chose for his Barrel + Beam "six pack" are two of the brewery's most popular brews: **Pret** (ABV 4.9 percent), a grisette beer, and **Terre à Terre** (ABV 6.5 percent), a saison. The former was traditionally served to Belgian miners, the latter to farm workers. Low in alcohol and light in body, Pret uses Michigan barley, wheat (which gives a creamy mouth-feel), and spelt (a wheat-like grain noted for tangy, nutty flavors). Barrel-aged, it has citrusy and tropical fruit notes which make it, Nick noted, "our answer to hazy IPAs." Terre à Terre, which Nick describes as a classic saison, departs from the local ingredients profile. European pilsner malt and Munich malt, along with Belgian wheat malt, create a full-bodied, rich beer to which are added dark fruit and citrus notes from the Aramis and Strisselspalt hops from France. The yeasts contribute funky, peppery notes. Bottle conditioned, it has an effervescence which balances the full body.

Tart (ABV 5 percent) and **Bliss** (ABV 5 percent) are both barrel-aged saisons. Tart is a biere de coupage, a French style from the nineteenth century that blends young, fresh, hoppy beer with mature barrel-aged beer. It is a crisp, dry, smooth beer that starts sweet, transitions into tartness, and then finishes dry. Bliss is a kellerbier, which is cold-lagered in oak barrels and carbonated with Michigan beet sugar. It has both a lager-like crispness and a tart finish.

Two of Barrel + Beam's "flavor added" beers use distinctly Michigan ingredients. **Sahti** (ABV 6.7 percent) is a beer that was popular with early Finnish settlers. Rye malt gives a spicy nip to the beer, while the Brewer's Gold hops provide a black current fruit flavor. The wort is filtered through fresh Michigan juniper boughs, which provide a bitterness, into a trough known as a kuurna. Sweet banana flavors are balanced by the spiciness and bitterness of the juniper and hops. **Spooky Kriek** (ABV 6 percent) uses Michigan cherries to add to the flavor and alcoholic content of a Belgian-style lambic. In fact three pounds are added to each gallon of liquid. The kriek goes through several stages of fermentation, beginning with the initial wild fermentation of the lambic. It's a very tart beer that one experienced imbiber described as being like a gose on steroids.

Barrel + Beam's farmhouse and other European style beers may initially strike someone who is used to drinking mainstream mass-produced lagers or even the standard range of craft beers as unusual. But where they are sipped gently and savored, their subtle blend of flavors come through, offering nuances never found in lawnmower beers or even in some craft beers.

⑭ Upper Peninsula Brewing Company

Upper Peninsula Brewing Company
(photo courtesy Upper Peninsula Brewing Company)

Address: 342 Rail St, Negaunee, MI 49866
Phone: 906-475-8722,
www.upperpeninsulabrewingcompany.com
www.facebook.com/UPbrewingcompany

By the middle of the twentieth century, both Negaunee and Ishpeming were in decline. Negaunee was particularly hard-hit as there was not only economic, but also literal depression. The mining tunnels that ran underground beneath the city made many buildings vulnerable to cave-ins. Areas were declared off limits and people were required to leave their homes and businesses; many buildings were demolished. After declining each decade since 1940, the population of the city rose in 2020 by just under one hundred. This modest increase was a tiny indication that vitality was increasing, particularly in the inner city. Much of it had to do with the celebration of its past. A cluster of shops brought antique lovers from across the Upper Peninsula and beyond; parks and museums were created; old buildings were reclaimed, renovated, and repurposed.

One of the restored buildings, which had been erected in the late nineteenth century and had been a meat processing and packing plant and later a furniture warehouse and showroom, had been turned into a brewery. Upper Peninsula Brewing Company, named after the last brewery in town, which had ceased operations before

Prohibition, was one of several restoration projects undertaken by long-time Negaunee residents Ann and Jim Kantola. They'd turned an old railroad station house into a vacation rental home, another building into a bar and grill, and another into an event center. Ann Kantola stated that these were buildings "that had history attached to them, that could be made current, and could be put to new use."

They had earlier wanted to convert another building into a brewery, but the city determined that it was unsafe and had it torn down. A couple of years later, they acquired the meatpacking/furniture structure. It was stripped down to the original brick walls and beams. The inoperable manual elevator that had been used to hoist carcasses was left intact as a reminder of the building's past. A comfortable taproom was created. Another part of the building contained the 3.5 barrel brewing system. Upper Peninsula Brewing would become a gathering place not only for the local people, but also for antique hunters, museum visitors, and hikers along the Iron Ore Heritage Trail, which ran in front of the building.

As has been the case with many of the recently opened craft breweries, simply serving beer in a welcoming taproom in a building with history was not enough. Since the Vierling Restaurant opened the Marquette Harbor Brewing half a century earlier, the county's beer drinkers, along with the growing number of tourists who visited the area, had become very knowledgeable about craft beers and very discriminating. Beers had to be not just different from mainstream industrial lagers. They had to be good and interesting.

New craft breweries needed a brewer who was both skilled and experienced. The Kantolas found one in Erica Tieppo, a native of the greater Detroit area who had studied at the Siebel Institute in Chicago and worked in breweries in Michigan, North Carolina, and Colorado. It was in the Rocky Mountain state that she had become a part owner of a brewery and oversaw the operation of its taproom. "I'd heard about the opening in Negaunee from friends who worked at Upper Hand in Escanaba and Blackrocks in Marquette. I was able to get back to Michigan, have an opportunity to oversee the creation of a new brewery, and enjoy one of my outdoor passions, sled dog racing." She would leave Upper Peninsula Brewing in February 2023.

I sat in the taproom with Mason Mathis, her chief assistant in the brewhouse , and talked about the beers they were creating. Mason, a home brewer who had moved to Marquettte recently and applied for a job at the new brewery, was, Erica told me later, an extremely enthusiastic and quick learner who was taking on more and more of the brewhouse duties and the development of recipes. He would become lead brewer after Tieppo's departure. While Upper Peninsula has created a variety of beers, they do for the most part, Erica said, "feature the synergy between the esters of Belgian ale yeasts and the varieties of hops that have been developed over the last decade or so." The esters provide notes of pears, plums and bananas; the hops, tropical and citrus flavors. "Our beers are," she emphasized, "very approachable and very drinkable."

The beers Mason chose for his "six pack," ranged from the relatively familiar Belgian Blonde to an unusual beer-wine hybrid called oenobeer. **Trail 8 Blonde Ale** (ABV 5 percent) they described as their entry-level beer. Light in body, not overly hoppy, easy-drinking, and crisp, it was given fruity notes from the Belgian yeast strain, a sweet maltiness from the Munich and Carafoam malts, and citrus and tropical fruit flavors along with spiciness and resiny tastes from a medley of hops. **Loop Garou Stout** (ABV 4.5 percent) takes its name from a stuffed figure found in the nearby Yooper Tourist Trap, a souvenir shop. The creature is supposed to be the preserved body of a supernatural creature feared by French Canadian loggers. Mason described the ale as "like Christmas chocolate-orange candy." Crystal and chocolate malts provided caramel and toffee flavors; wheat, a full-body; and orange peel and vanilla, hints of those Christmas candies.

Sunny Dew Hazy IPA (ABV 7 percent) takes its name from a Belgian yeast that provides spicy and stone fruit notes, while a medley of hops add citrusy, tropical, resinous, guava, and coconut hints. **Coppertown Amber Ale** (ABV 5.5 percent) uses Michigan Copper hops noted for their floral and Hawaiian fruit punch notes, along with roasted caramel malts to provide a robust ale that has some of the hoppiness of a pale ale or an IPA, with a fuller malt richness.

The final two beers of the six-pack are special in different ways. **Rose Eh Oenobeer** (ABV 7 percent) is a beer-wine hybrid in which the beer wort (from malted grains and hops) and the must (from crushed white wine grapes) are fermented simultaneously. Hibiscus, fruity hops, and the esters from Beglian yeasts provide a subtle and very unusual medley of flavors. **Golden Gurl**(ABV 7 percent), a strong Beglian ale, is the first Upper Peninsula recipe developed completely by Mason Mathis and seen through the brewing process entirely by himself. It combines the sweetness of agave, the spicy, ginger-like flavors of Grains of Paradise, and the sparkling quality of Hallertau hops to create a light and effervescent beer that has both citrus, tropical, and stone fruit flavors.

Old and new ingredients, old and new recipes result in the ideal beverages served in a new taproom in an old building that is part of an old city's strong efforts to renew itself.

⑮ Cognition Brewing Company

Cognition Brewing Company (photo by author)

Address: 113 East Canda St, Ishpeming, MI 49849
Phone: 906-204-2724,
www.cognitionbrewing.com
www.facebook.com/CognitionBrewingCompany

Like Negaunee, Ishpeming, five miles to the west, suffered from economic depression and loss of population during latter half of the twentieth century. And, also like Negaunee, one of the elements in the revitalization of the city in the second decade of the twenty-first century involved establishment of a craft brewery in a historic building—in this case a very well-known building that was on the National Register of Historic Places. In 2015, Cognition Brewing opened in the Mather Inn, which had been built in 1932 and, in 1959, had hosted the cast and crew of the motion picture *Anatomy of a Murder*. In fact the ground floor area that now housed Cognition's brewery and taproom had been the evening gathering place of such notables as James Stewart, George C. Scott, and Duke Ellington. There is a photograph in a corner of the taproom with Ellington seated at the piano and Stewart standing behind him, presumably singing (or humming) along. The Inn is flanked by two historic structures: the Grace Episcopal Church, built in 1901 is to the east, and the Carnegie Public Library, which opened in 1904, is to the west. To the south is a dive bar, the Rainbow Bar, which is famous because, in his retirement, John Voelker, author of novel *Anatomy of a Murder* (published under the pseudonym Robert Traver), used to spend frequent afternoons there playing cribbage with his cronies.

When I made my first visit to Cognition Brewery in the summer of 2017 to interview owner Jay Clancey and brewer Brian Richards, I noticed something missing that I'd seen in pictures of the entry to the taproom that had been taken in the previous winter. There were no mounds of snow blocking the doorway. It seems that the owners of the building had decided that Clancey was delinquent in paying his share of the power bills and dumped a truck-load of snow in front of the entry. Clancey was found not guilty of the accusations, the snow was removed, and for a while there existed an uneasy peace between owners and tenant.

Clancey, a local businessman who had discovered craft beer while living in Washington state, had wanted to help the city in its rejuvenation efforts and decided to set up a craft brewery in the downtown area. Although the Mather Inn had not been his first choice, it had the space for a cozy taproom, one with lots of history, and room for a brewhouse behind it. He invited Brian Richards, a home brewer for twelve years who had worked at Blackrocks Brewery, to be his lead brewer. "I'd tried his homebrew," Clancey remembered. "It was very good and I knew he had the experience."

It was Richards who came up with the name for the brewery: "Cognition." He told me: "When I tried Bells' Two Hearted Ale, a light went on. It was the first beer I tasted that had that much hops. Whenever my friends and I would try new and different beers, we wanted to know what makes this beer taste this way. I'd be filled with curiosity. And I had to learn how to make it." Cognition, the act of thinking, knowing and understanding, could be applied to drinking the beer Richards and his assistant Kris Thompson created. Don't just chug; sip and think about the complexities, the nuances of flavors you experience. If you wanted drinkers to think, you had to create a variety of interesting beers. By the time of my 2017 visit, Brian and Kris had done just that. Looking over a printout I'd made a few weeks earlier, I counted thirty different styles in the fifty-six different beers they'd created.

By the time of my return visit, in the summer of 2022, there had been a lot of changes. In fact, when I was doing background research in the very early spring, it seemed that the biggest change would be that there was no Cognition Brewing at all. The previous year, the landlords again complained that Cognition wasn't contributing its share to the power bill. This time, they didn't pile snow in front of the door; they disconnected power to the brewery. Clancey hooked up a generator to a power supply at Grace Episcopal Church, but the Mather Inn owners unplugged it and reportedly struck a brewery employee. Thousands of dollars of beer were spoiled and it appeared as if Cognition, if it were ever to reopen, would do so elsewhere. The owners were found guilty of contempt of court and the building was put up for sale. Suddenly, on the morning of April 1, 2022, Clancey announced that Cognition would reopen that afternoon—in the Mather Inn. "People thought it was an April Fools' joke," Clancey recalled. Instead, it was a wonderful April Fools surprise.

Before the reopening, Clancey was active on other fronts. He purchased the Episcopal Church building—the congregation was declining, but it would have the use of the space for Sunday worship. At other times, the building would be used as a social and events center. Clancey had taken another step in his work at helping to rejuvenate downtown Ishpeming. He also leased space in a building being repurposed on Marquette's Third Street and was turning it into a second brewery, Kognisjon Bryggeri. In the brewhouse, Kris Thompson had assumed the duties of head brewer, Brian Richards having taken a job as head brewer at a Lower Peninsula Brewery.

When I arrived at the brewery, the road running beside it was closed. A large party tent had been set up, with picnic tables under it and along the sidewalk. I learned that the next day, Cognition was to celebrate the renewal of an annual charity event that had been interrupted because of the pandemic and then the landlord troubles. The event would be the release of a special beer that would be named after the pet of whoever had won the bidding for the right to have their pet's name chosen. This year, the dog's name was Merle, and the beer, a German pilsner, was named Working Dog Blues. This year, for the first time, the beer would be canned;

Merle's picture would be on the front. Three dollars of every six pack, along with the money from the winning bid, would be donated to UPAWS, the Upper Peninsula Animal Welfare Shelter. "Over the years, we've raised thirty thousand dollars for the animal shelter," Jay told me.

Inside, the picture of Duke Ellington and Jimmy Stewart was still in its place; there were photographs of bicycles on other walls (the brewery supported RAMBA, the local mountain bike association), and above the bar were colorful posters with the names of the beers on tap. Although there was a new head brewer, the humor and creativity of naming was still alive and thriving. There was Psycbient All Zemba IPA, Visible Faeries Wheat Beer, Mork Borg Smoked Stout, and Near Death Saison, along with the three original beers, Gnome Wrecker Wheat Beer, Bloody Scream Cream Ale (a version of Deep Scream Cream Ale), and Oblivion Milk Stout.

Jay Clancey, who is an electrician by trade, had been helping the operators of the canning line correct some glitches. Returning to the taproom, he suggested we sit in a booth next to one of the larger windows in the place. "During the pandemic, when people couldn't come inside, we used to open this window and hand growlers and crowlers out to them." He remarked that between the pandemic and the obstacles thrown in his way by the landlords it had been a rough few years. "But it was worth hanging on. The loyalty of the community was wonderful; the support they gave us made us want to come back to this place." The vision that had led him to open a brewpub in Ishpeming still shone brightly. "There are lots of tourists; but the locals are so important, the people who live here. They walk or bike here for a beer or two. It brings them downtown. Since we first opened, we've seen several new businesses start up in the area."

Jay went back to the brewhouse to check on the canning process. Kris Thompson joined me to talk about his early beer experiences and the beers he was creating at Cognition. When he and his friends were in high school, they acquired a six pack of Sierra Nevada Torpedo, a 7.2 percent ABV, highly-hoped IPA. "We had trouble getting through it, since it was so much stronger and hoppier than anything we'd had before." They turned to stouts, using homebrew kits to create their own. Kris was involved with the formation of the Marquette Home Brewers group and served as president. "I knew Brian, and I'd bought a home in Ishpeming. When Cognition was getting going, I hung around, helping when I could and doing some bartending. Brian put me on the one-barrel system where I did test brews and experimental beers." Remembering what Brian had told me years earlier and the names and styles of the beers listed above the bar, I wasn't surprised when he described the Cognition house style as "experimental." In his words: "We make beer to think about. In fact, people search us out to try new beers. We even have someone visit us each year from Missouri; he travels to try our new beers." Part of the experimental nature involves foraging for (or buying at the market) local ingredients, including juniper, rhubarb, spruce tips, and mushrooms.

The first three beers produced by Cognition are relatively "normal," if by normal we mean that they were styles familiar to most craft beer drinkers. **Gnome Wrecker Belgian Pale Ale**(ABV 5.9 percent), the brewery's top-selling beer, is light-to-medium bodied, clean, and easy-drinking, with a firm malt background and a subtle funkiness imported by the yeast. Orange peel adds citrusy notes, Grains of Paradise peppery ones, and coriander a spiciness. **Oblivion Milk Stout** (ABV 5 percent) is an English style stout, with chocolate, coffee, and vanilla flavors. Lactose provides a creamy texture. **Bloody Scream Cream Ale** (ABV 5 percent) is a variation of the original Deep Scream Cream Ale with blood orange puree added. Designed as an entry-level beer, it is crisp and clean, with hints of orange fruit.

Pilsners have, over the past decade, become staples in the standard craft beer menu, but, recently, with a difference. Instead of just the usual German and Czech varieties with their noble hops, brewers are often creating variations using new and different hops and different yeasts. Cognition's **Fjordlands** (ABV 5 percent) uses Green Bullet hops from New Zealand that have flavors of fruits, pine needles, and spices, while Lutra Kveik yeast from Norway imparts a clean and crisp mouth feel. This is not a gentle, subtle pilsner, it's a full-flavored beverage. Drinking it will lead you up fjords to new "countries" of pilsner experience—and that's certainly consistent with the philosophy of the people at Cognition.

Graven-Tosk Gravol (ABV 6 percent), named after a "funeral beer" in a European board game, is a smoked stout using malts from Europe. The taste of the smoked malts is followed up by an unusual juniper taste. Thick, full-bodied and rounded, this unusual drink is not for people who are "afraid of the dark" in their beers.

Sahti is an ancient Finnish drink that some Upper Peninsula brewers are introducing not just to the many Finnish descendants in the area, but to beer aficionados who like to explore relatively unfamiliar ales and lagers. The wort for Cognition's **Midnattsol Sahti** (ABV 7.4 percent) is strained through freshly-foraged spruce boughs into a hollowed out aspen log, a kuurna. Rye malts contribute a spiciness and the yeast, banana notes.

Like nearly every other UP brewery, Cognition has its version of the "Official UP Beer," a blueberry ale. But, not surprisingly, it's not like the ones brewed by most other UP breweries. **Pombluegenesis Kettle Sour** (ABV 5.5 percent) is a Berliner weisse style wheat beer that uses both pomegranates and blueberries as flavor additives. It pours purple, has a slight tartness, a fruit aroma, and a dryness imported by the pomegranates. Not your everyday combination!

Several weeks after visiting Cognition and then sitting on the dock of the bay sipping and making notes about their beer, I was amazed at how extensive my tasting notes were—notes on three beers covered two or three reporter's notebook pages, more than what I fill for most beers, which would certainly prove that Cognition's brews really are beers for thought.

⑯ Jasper Ridge Brewery and Restaurant

Jasper Ridge Brewery and Restaurant (photo by author)

Address: 1705 Country Lane, Ishpeming, MI 49849
Phone: 906-485-6017,
www.jasperridgebrewery.com,
www.facebook.com/JasperRidgeBrewery

Jasper Ridge Brewery and Restaurant is located in Jasper Ridge Country village, a complex of shops, restaurants, hotels, and offices north of Michigan 28, which bypasses the centers of Negaunee and Ishpeming. It isn't in a historic building, but, in the story of the Upper Peninsula's craft beer movement, it does have historical significance. It opened in 1996, the fifth brewpub to start up in the Upper Peninsula. It was designed to serve shoppers, workers in Jasper Ridge Country Village, tourists staying at a nearby RV park, and the hotels in the complex, as well as travelers passing along Highway 28 and area residents out to enjoy a lunch or dinner.

A succession of brewers has created the beers and ales that have complemented patrons' meals. The first of these was Grant Lyke, an area home brewer who would later set up brewhouses for the Bayou Brewery and then the Lake Superior Steakhouse Brewpub in

Harvey, just south of Marquette. I met Grant when I first visited Jasper Ridge in 2011. He described the beers he created as balanced. "I follow style guidelines carefully. I want something that is very drinkable for the average customer." At first, that meant brewing something that was mild and low-hopped to serve as an entry-level beer. "But people have evolved and they're now much more knowledgeable about craft beers. They're willing to try something new." One of the first beers he brewed, Ropes Golden Wheat, is still on the menu and is Jasper Ridge's best-seller.

After Grant Lyke moved on, a series of brewers took over. When I talked to one of them, Matt Buelling, who would later move to become Drifa's first lead brewer, the words "approachable" and "drinkable" came up. Several of the beers I'd been introduced to on my first visit were still on the menu, although each brewer had tweaked the recipes. He also noted that, as customers' knowledge of craft beer increased, the brewers added new beers.

On my summer 2022 visit, the brewing was done by a committee, some of whom were veteran home brewers. They were led by Kevin Hokenson, Jasper Ridge's general manager. We chatted, sitting at a table near the brewhouse, whose ten-barrel system seemed very large for such a relatively small brewery, one that produces only a few hundred barrels a year. "We fill up the tanks regularly for Golden Ropes and Wayward Blonde, our big sellers, and our blueberry beer," Kevin told me. "For the other beers, particularly the rotating ones, we make smaller batches."

Kevin began his discussion of the "six pack" of Jasper Ridge beers with the two entry-level "stepping-stone" beers. **Wayward Blonde Ale** (ABV 5 percent) "is the one we offer people who have been used to drinking beers like Pabst Blue Ribbon or Bud Light. It's a basic beer, very lightly-hopped and with Vienna malts that give a biscuit flavor." It is the base beer for **Cherry Blonde Ale** (ABV 5 percent). **Rope's Golden Wheat** (ABV 5 percent), named after a nearby goldmine, uses red and white wheat malt. It's crisp and clean, with some maltiness and, he noted, is a favorite with people used to drinking Labatt's Blue and Blue Moon. It is the base beer for **Blastin' Blueberry Wheat** (ABV 5 percent), named after the regular explosions at the mine.

Bonfire Smoked Porter (ABV 7 percent) and **Copper Kolsch** (ABV 4.9 percent) move beyond the stepping-stone classification. The former, which is lightly hopped, uses smoked malts to create a beverage that has coffee, chocolate, and caramel notes. Medium-bodied, it is, Kevin noted, going to remind outdoor-loving patrons of a campfire. The latter, brewed in the true German style, uses pilsner malts and noble hops to create a beer that is clean, crisp and delicate. The spiciness of the hops is balanced by the bready and slightly sweet malt background.

Jasper Ridge has also offered several of the different kinds of India Pale Ales over the years. **Double Frozen Auger Imperial Pale Ale** (ABV 8.2 percent), which Kevin described as loaded with "C" hops—Cascade, Centennial, Columbus—is named after what happened to an essential part for an ice-cleaning Zamboni machine operated by a member of the brewing team. It has heavy citrus and grapefruit flavors and finishes dry and clean. **Attack Penguin IPA** (ABV 6.8 percent) uses Chinook, Centennial and Pekko hops that create an interesting medley of floral, pine, and citrus flavors.

As I sat sipping a glass of Rope's Golden Wheat and enjoying a delicious Italian cudighi sandwich, I thought that my final stop on this ale trail had also been the beginning for many locals' journey into the "land" of craft beer. Here, in the second-oldest brewery in Marquette county, one housed in a very modern building, many Yoopers first discovered craft beer styles that were often over a century old. It was "stepping-stone" brews like Ropes and Wayard Blonde that introduced many people to what craft beer could be like. The introductions made it possible for beginning beer drinkers to advance to enjoying the much more complex beers that they would later experience.

Copper Harbor, Calumet
Houghton, South Range

At the same time that iron mining began in the Ishpeming-Marquette area, copper mining started on the Keweenaw Peninsula. Before more profitable mines were developed in western Montana and southern Arizona, the UP copper mining industry flourished well into the twentieth century. As happened in many boom towns in nineteenth-century America, several breweries, most of them owned by brewers trained in Germany, sprung up in Michigan's copper country. Only one of these, Bosch Brewing Company, continued to operate after the repeal of Prohibition. In the 1950s, it produced 100,000 barrels of beer, making it one of the state's larger breweries. Although it was distributed far beyond its Hancock headquarters, it was a local favorite and an integral part of the community. In 1968, it even created a "sauna beer," based on a Finnish recipe, as a salute to the legions of families that had moved from Finland at the height of the mining boom. Unable to compete with the larger regional breweries and enormous national ones,

Bosch ceased operations in 1973. Empty bottles with Bosch labels are eagerly sought after items in antique stores in the UP.

The copper mining boom long over, the Keweenaw Peninsula is now the home to two universities, Michigan Technological University and Finlandia University, several small industries, service businesses, and four craft breweries. In 1997, the Library Restaurant in Houghton obtained a craft beer license. In 2004, three decades after the closing of Bosch Brewing left the Upper Peninsula without a production brewery, Keweenaw Brewing Company began operations in Houghton, serving product in their downtown taproom/brewery and distributing product across the Upper Peninsula. In 2005, Michigan House Café began brewing its own beer under the name Red Jacket Brewing. The fourth brewery, Brickside in Copper Harbor, opened for business in 2012.

⑰ Brickside Brewery

Brickside Brewery (photo by author)

Address: 64 Gratiot St, Copper Harbor, MI 49918
Phone: 906-289-4772
www.bricksidebrewery.com

In the middle of the nineteenth century, Copper Harbor, located at
the northern tip of the Keweenaw Peninsula, became one of the
important centers of the copper mining era. It was the site of Fort
Wilkins, which was active from 1844 to 1846 and from 1867 to
1870, and a port from which much of the ore extracted from
nearby mines was shipped. However, the town's fortunes declined
in the later part of the nineteenth century as the mining focus
shifted south toward Calumet and Houghton. It is now an
"unincorporated community" with a year-around population,
according to the 2020 census, of 136. The local economy is based
on tourism and, for beer tourists, the attraction is Brickside
Brewery, which, in 2012 became the first brewery to operate in
Keweenaw County since Eagle River Brewery closed its doors in the
late 1880s.

When I first visited Brickside in 2017, I noticed three things: the traffic moved slowly down the main street and many of the vehicles had kayaks on their roofs or bicycles on rear racks. This was definitely a destination for outdoor lovers. Across the street from the taproom was a beer distributor's truck with a big sign for Fat Tire, a craft beer made in Colorado, on its side. The products of the very large craft breweries had reached this tiny outpost of northern Michigan. The modest sign identifying Brickside and attached to a large pole reminded me of the sign for an unassuming English pub in a little country village. Certainly, Brickside wasn't out to compete with the big boys.

The low-ceilinged taproom is small. The walls are covered with stickers from other craft breweries; there is the copper-topped bar with a half-dozen stools in front of it and a few tables and chairs scattered about. Beside one wall is a popcorn machine with cardboard containers and a plastic jar for one-dollar donations (on the honor system) next to it. Through the window in a door along another wall can be seen the three-barrel brewing system. The most interesting feature of the taproom is the wall to the right of the front door. The plaster has been scraped away and on each of the exposed bricks is a person's name, or in some cases, a couple's or family's name. As part of a fundraising campaign to help finance the new brewery, patrons could make a five-dollar donation and write their names on a brick. Over three hundred bricks have been signed. This is how the brewery got its name.

I sat at the end of the bar with Jason Robinson, brewer and, with his wife Jessica, co-owner of Brickside. His story was a not unfamiliar one. He was not a Yooper, but had married one: his wife was a Copper Harbor native and her family owned the store in front of which the truck with the Fat Tire sign had parked. Jason, who grew up in Milwaukee, had not been a fan of any beers and had only discovered craft beer when he sampled some of the beers from his in-laws' store. A sister-in-law had given him a home brewing kit as a Christmas gift, and he became interested in the brewing process. Noticing the growing volume of tourist trade at the tip of the Keweenaw Peninsula, he thought a brewery and taproom would be a good idea. He took an online course from the American Brewers Guild and then interned at the Jolly Pumpkin Brewery in Dexter, Michigan. The brewery and taproom opened in 2012.

Jason described the beers he created at Brickside as middle-of-the-road, although, he added, "We do some saisons and Belgian wits. Once we did a stout with cardamom seasoning and Turkish coffee. We offer a standard range of styles and, because we have a small brewing system (three barrels), we can tinker with our recipes and make small tweaks. Next year our styles may taste a little different and have new names. We can't do lagers—we don't have enough tank space."

I didn't try any samples as I had a long and winding road ahead of me, so I decided to buy a few bomber bottles to take along. Unfortunately, he only had an IPA in the beer cooler, but suggested I cross the street to his in-laws' store. "It will only take you a couple of minutes to get there; it takes the beer a lot longer." Because of distribution laws, he had to sell his product to a distributor located in the town of Chassell, an hour and fifteen minutes drive to the south. It would then be shipped back to Copper Harbor. These arcane laws were changed a few years later, but by that time Jason no longer bottled and distributed his beer.

When I dropped by Brickside in 2022, there were more names on the wall inside the door, but not the names of donors, just of people wanting to leave a record of their having passed through. The beers listed on the chalkboard behind the bar had different names, but there seemed to be a range of styles similar to what I'd noticed on the earlier visit. Jason was busy brewing, but was able to take a quick break and discuss some of the listed beers. **Fine Day Pale Ale** (ABV 5 percent) has citrusy and floral notes. **Some IPA** (ABV 6.5 percent) is a West Coast version of the style. Mosaic and Cascade hops contribute a variety of floral, tropical fruits and earthy notes. Jason noted that the local Copper Harbor water system took the edge off the bitterness that is often a characteristic of the style. **Up Hill Both Ways Double IPA** (ABV 8.8 percent) he called a balanced beer with the Willamette hops providing floral and fruit notes and the Hallertau hops, a spiciness.

I was delighted to see two of my favorite styles: Extra Special Bitter and Saison. Several decades ago on a trip to England, I'd first tasted an ESB and discovered that beers didn't have to be as bland as the ubiquitous North American Pale Lagers. **Jackpine Savage ESB** (ABV 5.2 percent) uses Golden Promise and Crystal 60 malts which create a slightly sweet, but robust caramel and toffee flavor. The Progress hops are grassy and minty. Over two decades ago, I experienced the wonderfully funky and peppery qualities of saisons. Brickside's **Farm Beer** (ABV 4.6 percent) didn't disappoint. "I just let the yeasts do all their crazy stuff," was Robinson's succinct description of his saison. The last of his "six pack" was **Red Metal Amber** (ABV 5 percent), an ale given a spicy zing by the rye malts included in the grain bill.

It was time for Jason to return to the brewhouse. I chatted briefly with some of the patrons, one couple who had a summer cabin on a nearby lake and were in town on their weekly grocery trip, the other part of a group overnighting before taking the passenger ferry to Isle Royale, a four-hour voyage to the northwestern part of Lake Superior. As frequently happens on my beer travels, we chatted about craft beer and recommended to each other the favorite pubs and taprooms we'd visited.

⑱ Red Jacket Brewing Company at Michigan House Café

Red Jacket Brewing Company (photo by author)

Address: 300 Sixth St, Calumet, MI 49913;
Phone: 906-337-1910
www.michiganhousecafe.com

My visit to Brickside over, I headed south toward Calumet, pausing a couple of times to notice two very interesting signs. The first, at the western edge of Copper Harbor, marks the northern terminus of US Highway 41 and posts the distance to Miami, Florida, the southern terminus: 1990 miles. The second, a half-hour down the road, is what has been dubbed the "Snow Thermometer," an enormous pole on which are marked the annual snowfall levels. The lowest mark was 161 inches above the ground, the highest 394 inches.

Calumet, originally known as Red Jacket, had been the elegant business center for the Keweenaw copper industry. A large number of the wonderful old buildings, several of them churches, are still around, but, sadly, many are empty and in disrepair. The city, population now just over six hundred, is part of the Keweenaw

National Historical Park, with buildings and notable sites preserved and celebrated and some undergoing restoration. The Fire Hall has been turned into a history museum, and an old church is now an art theatre. The Calumet Theatre, which opened in 1900, still operates.

My destination was in the center of town at a building that was well over a century old and had, over two decades ago, been restored and turned into a restaurant/brewpub: Red Jacket Brewing Company at the Michigan House Café. The building, which had been created in 1905 as a saloon/restaurant/hotel by the Bosch Brewing Company, had been vacant for several years when it was bought in 2001 by Tim and Sue Bies, who had moved from the Lower Peninsula to be closer to their son, a student at Michigan Technological University in Houghton.

A few months after the purchase, the Bies opened the building as a restaurant, one which featured a full bar that included popular import beers, along with some by the mega American brewers. Tim and his son were home brewers and decided that providing good beer brewed on the premises would be a complement to the first class meals the kitchen was concocting. In 2005, they opened Red Jacket Brewing Company.

Neither of the Bies, nor the current brewer, Brian Hess was able to meet with me when I visited in 2017. But I was able to enjoy my dinner, along with a sampler tray of beers, and gaze around at the restored/renovated restaurant. It was a long, narrow room, with booths along the wall, a few tables, and a bar. The windows were decorated with some vintage stained glass; taxidermist specimens of game animals, birds, and fish decorated the walls, along with old saws, and a fishing rod. On the ceiling, a number of snowshoes made tracks across the plaster. Near the bar was a big, boxy old-fashioned television; on the bar an even more old-fashioned, manually operated cash register. The highlight of the room was the mural above the large mirrors behind the bar. Original to the building, it depicted an outdoor festival with the celebrants enjoying good food and beer; in the center was the coat of arms of the original Bosch brewery. While the appearance was different, the ambiance reminded me of the Vierling Saloon in Marquette, with its early twentieth-century feel and artifacts.

When I visited again in June 2022, it was a Wednesday and the restaurant was not open. As I sat with brewer Brian Hess in the dimly lit and quiet empty dining area, I had a sense of having been transported into the past when the art and artifacts were new. Brian talked about his background and how he had come to take over the brewing duties at Red Jacket. He is an engineering graduate from Pennsylvania State University who developed a taste for craft beer from Yuengling Brewery, which had been established in 1829, and the much newer Boston and Sierra Nevada brewing companies. A home brewer, he moved to Calumet to work for a local electronics firm and spent much of his leisure time hanging around Red Jacket talking about beer with Bies and his son. He began helping in the brewhouse and gradually assumed full-time duties, brewing relatively small batches every other Saturday.

Several years ago, Tim Bies had commented that Michigan House Café was "a restaurant that made its own beer." Patrons could purchase growlers to take with them, but enjoying beer on the premises was seen as part of the Michigan House Café experience. One of the favorites is **Oatmeal Express Stout** (ABV 6.5 percent), Red Jacket's first beer and its bestseller. A stout flavored with "lots of espresso," it is a dry, smooth ale, given a rich flavor from the espresso and the Maris Otter malts and an earthiness from the Fuggle hops. **Downtown Brown Ale** (ABV 6 percent) also uses Maris Otter Malts and Fuggle hops. A middle-of-the-road American version of the style, it is a smooth, mildly hopped, medium-bodied brew. **Keweenaw Cowboy IPA** (ABV 7.5 percent) strikes a balance between the sweetness of the Munich malts and the spicy, cirtusy, zesty notes of the Mt. Hood, Cascade and Citra hops. **Smooth Trail Pale Ale** (ABV 7 percent) is a stronger-than-usual rendition of the style, but is approachable, and easy drinking.

Two of the Red Jacket beers have interesting back stories. The first, **Shot Rock Wee Heavy Scotch Ale** (ABV n/a), was created at the request of the organizers of a local bonspiel, a curling tournament. A full-bodied, dark ale with caramel and chocolate malts, it was so popular that it has become a regular offering. The second, **Syla Belgian Tripel** (ABV 7.3 percent), was created as part of a worldwide brewers' response to the Russian invasion of the Ukraine. Pravda Beer Theatre of Lliv invited brewers to make a donation to the relief fund in exchange for the rights to brew their Syla beer. Light on hops, it has roasted caramel notes along with coriander and peppercorn. Candy sugar, which is used in the fermentation process, helps increase the alcohol content while keeping the ale fairly light-bodied.

⑲ Copper Country Brewing Company at the Library Restaurant

Copper Country Brewing Company (photo by author)

Address: 62 Isle Royale St, Houghton, MI 49931
Phone: 906-481-2665,
www.thelibraryhoughton.com,
www.facebook.com/thelibraryhoughton

The drive from Calumet to Houghton goes past the Quincy Mine complex, now an historical site offering tours of a mine shaft and old buildings, down a steep hill through Hancock, across the Portage Lake Lift Bridge (much, much shorter than the Mackinac Bridge, but nonetheless very impressive) and up another steep hill into downtown Houghton, one of the three places in the Upper Peninsula where there is only a short walk between two breweries, in this case between the Copper Country Brewing at the Library Restaurant and the taproom of Keweenaw Brewing Company.

I stopped first at the Library Restaurant located on Isle Royale Street, a very steep road leading down to the water. The building that housed it had been built near the end of the nineteenth century and had been a cabinet shop and embalming "parlor" before it became a restaurant shortly before the beginning of World War I. In1967, it had been rechristened The Library and, in 1998, after it had been seriously damaged by a fire and extensively restored and renovated, reopened as a brewpub, the last of the six UP brewpubs that had opened in the six years after the Michigan law change. The business was sold in 2018 to Tom Romps, owner of another local restaurant, who renamed the brewery Copper Country Brewing, "In honor of the Copper Country Strong and the strength of this community thru the devastating events of the Father's Day Flood, 2018."

I'd visited the Library in 2017, but hadn't been able to meet with then owner Jim Cortright or brewer Bob Jackson. I sipped a couple of beer samples, gazed at the shelves and shelves of books lining the brick walls. The titles didn't seem that interesting—I guess they were of the "look but don't read" variety. What I most remember was the wonderful view of the Portage Canal and the steep hill of Hancock that I could see from the picture windows looking north. The five-barrel brewhouse was fitted snugly into the corner of the dining room, and it too had a fantastic view of the water, even better than the view enjoyed by Chumley Anderson, the brewer at the Vierling in Marquette.

On my 2022 visit, I met with Bob Jackson who, I learned, was in the final few months of his quarter-of-a-century career as the chief brewer at the Library. A native of Duluth who was a member of a family of home brewers, he had discovered craft beer when he first enjoyed San Francisco's Anchor Steam Beer and Porter. He'd come to Houghton to do graduate work at Michigan Technological University and, when he discovered that a brewer was needed at the recently reopened Library, he applied and was accepted. Now, he was training Christian Maki, the owner's son-in-law, as his successor. "I'm going to enjoy riding my bike in the good weather, skiing in the winter, and reading," he told me, although he did admit that he'd look forward to coming back to the Library, not to gather reading material, but to enjoy a pint of his successor's beer.

Jackson has created beers that range from the very light **Rock Harbor Light Ale** (ABV 3.8 percent) to **Devil's Washtub Double IPA** (ABV 8.2 percent). Fruit beers are very popular, he said, and included apricot, peach passion fruit, raspberry, and mango. Of course, there's a blueberry beer, **Rice Lake Blueberry Ale** (ABV 4.5 percent). **Rock Harbor Light Ale** is what Bob calls "the baby brother of our pale ale." It's a balanced session ale with a noticeable, but not overwhelming taste of hops. The big brother, **Husky Pale Ale** (ABV 5.9 percent), is an American style of pale ale, with Cascade hops contributing grapefruit, piney, and floral notes.

The Copper Country beer menu lists several of what might be called "colored" beers. **Red Ridge Rye Ale** (ABV 4.7 percent) contains 15 percent rye malt, which gives a nip to the beer. The Chinook pops add spicy notes; the Northern Brewer hops, piney and minty flavors. **Copper City Gold** (ABV 4.5 percent) is an American wheat style, "a gentle wheat beer," Jackson calls it, "not overpowering, not over-hopped." Noble hops add a spiciness and Northern Brewer hops a piney, minty hint. **Bete Grise** (which means gray beast in French) is the name of a Keweenaw Peninsula nature preserve and also of Copper County's brown ale (ABV 5.5 percent). Dryer and less sweet than many popular English versions of the style, it is malty rich with coffee notes. "It's robust," Bob says, "not overwhelming." **White City Wheat** (ABV 5.6 percent) is a German style hefeweizen in which clove and banana notes imparted by the yeast are noted. **Rice Lake Blueberry Ale** (ABV 4.5) is a very low-hopped beer, which allows the flavor of the berries to stand out against the background of the Copper Country Gold Ale.

When Bob Jackson, one of the original six Upper Peninsula craft brewers, retires, the active pioneer craft brewers will be Lark Ludlow at Tahquamenon Falls and Chumley Anderson at the Vierling. But Christian Maki, the now apprentice, but soon-to-be head brewer at Copper Country Brewery, will carry on the legacy. You can check it out at the Library.

⑳ Keweenaw Brewing Company

Keweenaw Brewing Company (photo by author)

Taproom and brewery: 408 Shelden Ave, Houghton, MI 49931
Phone: 906-482-5596
Production brewery: 10 Fourth St, South Range, MI 49963
Phone: 906-482-1937
www.kbc.beer
www.facebook.com/keweenawbrewing

Half a block south on Isle Royale and then a block-and-a-half west on Shelden Avenue stands a building of historic significance to aficionados of craft beer. 408 Shelden Avenue is the home of the taproom and trial brewery of Keweenaw Brewing Company: the first craft brewery to open in the Upper Peninsula in the twenty-first century, the first Upper Peninsula production brewery since the demise of Bosch Brewing in 1973, and the first Michigan brewery to can its product.

Behind the windows of the taproom of KBC (as the locals fondly call the brewery) are displays relating to the area's brewing history. In one is a very old keg with the name "Bosch Brewing" stamped on it and beside it a six pack of stubbies from the 1970s. A pickaxe, shovel, and miner's lamp complete the display. In the other window are six packs of various KBC beers and samples of KBC swag-clothing, glasses, mementos, and a flag proclaiming: "Drink Local: It's Superior." There are two entrances: when the brewery opened in 2004, it became so popular so quickly that the owners took over the vacant commercial space next door. They opened an archway in the walls separating the two spaces, but left the two front doors. The right side of the building houses the 12-barrel brewing system, a few tables, and a bar, over which is a sign that admonishes: "Save the earth; it's the only planet with beer." There are more tables on the other side of the taproom, along with a lounge where easy chairs and sofas surround a gas-burning fireplace. During renovations, the walls were scraped back to reveal the original brick; stained glass windows that had been hidden behind the plaster have been rehung; repurposed lumber has been used where possible. A backdoor leads to a patio that overlooks Portage Lake. The famous Lift Bridge isn't visible, but it is depicted on a large mural covering the outside wall of an adjacent building.

It was in the bar area that, during my 2017 Circ-Ale tour, I met KBC's owners: Dick Gray and Paul Boissevain. The former, a native of Midland in the Lower Peninsula, had attended Michigan Technological University, just a few blocks down the road; the latter attended the University of California at Santa Cruz. The two, who both admitted to having consumed a great deal of "cheap beer" in college, had met, become friends, and discovered the burgeoning craft beer scene while working in the petroleum industry in Colorado.

One of their favorite watering holes was Wynkoop Brewery, which had opened in 1988, the first brewpub in the Rocky Mountain State. "Wouldn't it be great to have a brewpub like this in the Upper Peninsula?" Dick remembered thinking. "Houghton is a great town, there's a great university there, and wonderful outdoors just beyond the city. But it was hard to find craft beer in the area." He talked Boissevain into joining him in opening a brewery in the Upper Peninsula, and invited Dave Lawrence, one of the brewers at Wynkoop, to become the head brewer.

The creation of their envisioned brewery, which they would give a strong local identity with the name Keweenaw, was carefully planned out. They would need to start with a downtown location, somewhere with a waterfront view and not far from Michigan

Tech. The place would house both a small production facility and a taproom. A 12-barrel brewing system would enable them to create sufficient product to service both local patrons and area accounts. The kegs achieved an amusing popularity shortly after the brewery/taproom had opened in 2004. One of the clubs at the university put beer kegs on the list for a scavenger hunt. "We sold a lot of kegs," Paul chuckled. "And they bought them full!"

From the beginning, the taproom was considered a part of the community, "a third place" where locals and visitors could gather, engage in conversation, enjoy the view from the rear deck, and sip beer. Michigan Tech students of legal drinking age were hired to work in the taproom. Pints were priced at $2.50. "We wanted students and visitors to remember us after they left the area and to buy our beer when they found it in other places." Other places would increase to include all of the Upper Peninsula, most of the Lower Peninsula, and much of northern Wisconsin and northeastern Minnesota.

A large and separate production brewery was part of the long-range plan right from the start. In 2005, Paul and Dick found a large enough building in South Range, just ten minutes south of town. In 2006, they closed on the property, and a year later began production. Every year since 2004, when 460 barrels of beer were sold at the Shelden Avenue facility, production had increased. By 2008, the second full year of operation at the South Range plant, the figure had risen to 3240. "Our plan was to increase annual production to around 12,000 barrels; we never wanted to go much above that figure," Dick Gray told me. The 10,000-barrel mark was reached in 2014 and the 12,000 in 2018. Production has hovered around that mark since.

To achieve their production goals, they had to have not only good beer, but also beer that appealed to their chosen market area. The UP had six brewpubs when Keweenaw Brewing Company opened and a few craft beers from the Lower Peninsula and Wisconsin were available. However, Budweiser products and, to a lesser extent, others from Miller and Coors dominated the market. "We never wanted big beers [high in alcohol content], but sessional beers," Gray told me. "Big beers wouldn't work for cyclists, hikers, and other outdoors people who visit or are from this area. So we worked at creating moderate beers—not bland and not in your face." Their early beers, including Pick Axe Blonde, Red Jacket

Amber Ale, Lift Bridge Brown Ale, and Widow Maker Black Ale (at first called Tower Ale) were just that: all were around 5 percent ABV, light-to-medium-bodied, and flavorful.

In 2017, I'd briefly stopped at the South Range production facility to introduce myself to head brewer Tom Duex and to take a look at the facility that would in that year produce 11,384 barrels of beer. In 2022, I enjoyed a longer visit, talking at length with Duex about the KBC beers. As during my first visit, the brewhouse was, pardon the phrase, "a beer-hive of activity." A new batch of beer was being brewed, the canning line was working at full speed, a forklift was moving pallets of beer, shrink-wrapped in flats of 24 cans, to the cool room. Tom and I sought out a quiet space—the lounge just outside the business offices.

Tom, a native of nearby Dollar Bay, had been with KBC since the start, working on the renovations downtown and later on the building of the production facility. He'd been interested in beer since his teens. "It was difficult to find craft beer around here then. We'd go to grocery and party stores looking for European beers that might have been in stock. I liked tasting them and I really enjoyed trying to see what made each of them taste different. I was really interested in what various malts did." He worked as Dave Lawrence's assistant for two years and also took a course on brewing at Chicago's Siebel Institute of Technology before becoming the leader of the brewing team.

He began his discussion of KBC beers with a general statement about the KBC brewing philosophy. "We started making traditional beers. Our focus was on balance between hops and malts. There's a right way to use hops. More isn't always better. Hops have to help the final product. We respect each style and we're methodical, strict, and consistent. We try not to be too aggressive because we serve a wide range of beer drinkers; but most of them seem to prefer simple flavors. One thing we've discovered is that more and more people like fruit beers. They're hard to make, but the end result is worth it." Tom concluded by stating: "We want to make the best beer we can make in each category. We set high standards for ourselves."

The first three beers in the "six pack" Duex chose to discuss, the company's top sellers, also three of the first of their beers to go on the market. The label on cans of **Pick Axe Blonde** (ABV 4.7 percent) shows a buxom young lady dressed in the traditional garb of a server in a German beer hall. She is wielding a pick axe, that basic miner's tool, but is smiling invitingly. It's a simple, basic beer designed to welcome newcomers to the craft beer world. Clear and light-bodied, it has a simple malt body and a slight hop tang, what the advertising copy called "a kiss of hops." **Red Jacket Amber Ale** (ABV 5.1 percent) is like an Oktoberfest, with a Munich malt body and a sweetness that is balanced by the spiciness of German noble hops.

That **Widow Maker Black Ale** (ABV 5.2 percent) is the top selling of KBC's beer (over 40 percent of total sales each year) is somewhat surprising. In a land where Busch Light is the top-selling beer of all brands, Widow Maker is the complete opposite of that mass produced lager. Based on the German Schwarzbier (black beer) style, it's as dark as Busch is pale, and filled with coffee and molasses flavor along with just enough German hops to offset the sweetness. "If you can't finish a Widow Maker," Paul Boissevain told me, "you have a problem." On the back of the t-shirts worn by servers in the taproom is the slogan "Don't Be Afraid of the Dark." Judging by customer response, not many have been.

The next three beers, while less familiar to middle-of-the-road craft beer drinkers, are not highly unusual or aggressive in-your-face brews. **Point Trail Ale** (ABV 7 percent) has been variously called an American Pale Ale, a Rye Pale Ale, or an IPA. Cascade, Mosaic, and Citra hops contribute grapefruit, piney, floral, bubblegum and earthy notes; rye malt, a spicy crispness, and crystal malt, a caramel sweetness. "This beer has a lot going on for someone who likes higher malt and hop contributions," Duex commented. **Red Ridge Blood Orange Ale** (ABV 5.5 percent) is a clean, crisp beer in which the simple blonde ale provides a malt background to the sweetness and tartness of the blood orange puree. **Hefe Royale** (ABV 5 percent) is a German style wheat beer in which, Tom notes, "the yeast is the star." It's silky in texture, and clove and banana tastes are noticeable.

After my visit to the South Ridge production brewery, I noticed that in the beer coolers of the convenience and party stores I stopped at, the KBC "big three," along with others of their beers were nearly always in stock, and I remembered Dick Gray's statement that he and Paul Boissevain had created a hometown brewery and that the hometown was "all of the Upper Peninsula." That statement certainly seemed true. They'd gauged their market very well and created beers that steadily increasing numbers of "hometown" sippers have certainly enjoyed.

Ironwood, Marenisco,
Alpha, Kingsford

The 125 miles of US Highway 2 between Ironwood and Iron Mountain run through what was once the heart of the iron ore industry of the southwestern Upper Peninsula: the Gogebic Range to the west and the Menominee Range to the east. Near the various mine sites, towns grew and businesses thrived. However, mines began to close toward the middle of the twentieth century, businesses closed, and populations shrunk. For example, Ironwood's population dropped from 15,739 in 1920 to 5,045 a century later.

Although mine shafts were barred and buildings boarded up and houses became dilapidated, the natural beauties of the area remained: streams, brooks, waterfalls, and lakes; rolling hills covered with evergreens and hardwoods. So too did a smaller, but determined population. They would live in their cities, create businesses, and respond to the passages of the seasons in the landscapes around them. They would hunt and fish, hike, canoe, and bicycle, snowshoe and ski. And they would provide services for a growing number of tourists who would pass through, stay for a while, or even become summer residents.

One of the services they provided for themselves and the passers-through was the brewing of beer. There had been pre-Prohibition breweries in Ironwood and Bessemer in the west and Iron Mountain in the east, but no beer had legally been brewed in the area since 1933. That all changed in 2017, when Cold Iron Brewing opened in Ironwood, followed the next year by 51st State Brewing in Kingsford and Alpha Michigan Brewing in Alpha, and, in 2022, by Five Sons Brewing in Marenisco.

What is one of the most enjoyable aspects of visiting these microbreweries from Ironwood to Kingsford is that visitors must leave Highway 2 and wend their way through towns and villages. Cold Iron is just off the main street of Ironwood, a city that has for several years been restoring its downtown, making it an enjoyable destination for locals and visitors alike. Marenisco is a very small village south of the highway, as is Alpha. The creators of the breweries wanted not only to provide third places for their fellow townspeople to gather, but to invite visitors to enjoy local beer with them. When Jeff Brickey was seeking a location for his brewery, he chose a neighborhood in Kingsford that could best be reached by driving through residential areas of Iron Mountain.

㉑ Cold Iron Brewing

Cold Iron Brewing (photo by author)

Address: 104 South Lowell St, Ironwood, MI 49938
Phone: 906-285-7020,
www.coldironbrewing.com,
www.facebook.com/coldironbrewing

In 2017, I decided to drive into Ironwood from the west along
Business Route 2, which passed through Hurley, Wisconsin, one of
the "hell towns in the pines" during the later nineteenth century.
Driving down Hurley's Silver Street, I counted twenty bars and
taverns, some of them displaying large signs announcing that their
establishments featured "Hollywood Dancing Girls." Crossing the
Montreal River into Michigan, I missed the turn to Cold Iron
Brewing and enjoyed a brief tour of downtown Ironwood. I saw a
couple of bars, but no signs for dancing girls. What did catch my
attention were signs pointing to the Downtown Art Park, the
Downtown Art Place and the historic Ironwood Theatre. Circling
the block I noticed another sign pointing the direction to the Belle
Iron Trail, a part of the North Country Trail.

Seeing the signs reminded me of an article I'd read about a plan
the civic leaders of Ironwood had developed a decade or so ago to
make the downtown area more attractive to both the local citizens
and tourists who might otherwise pass by on the main route of

Highway 2 that ran north of the city. This plan was partly responsible for the creation in 2017 of Cold Iron Brewing, the first local brewery since the pre-Prohibition era. The idea was not only to provide parks, museums, art galleries and hiking trails, but also to encourage the opening of coffee shops, small restaurants, and a craft brewery as "third places" where friends and strangers could gather.

At around this time, John Garske and his wife, Lee-Ann, had spent many vacations visiting craft brewpubs and taprooms around the Midwest and had thought that opening one in downtown Ironwood would be very good idea. They gathered a group of interested friends and began planning. One of the people they talked to was Andy Warren, who also had a plan. "I was in a dead-end job and started making a business plan for a craft brewery. I'd been a home brewer, I really liked craft beer, and I wanted to get out of what I was doing. My wife is from here and through her I met John and his group."

The goals of the civic planners, Garske and his friends, and Warren coincided and Garske, friends, and Warren began taking steps to form a craft brewery and taproom in downtown Ironwood. They purchased a building that had housed administrative offices of the United States Forest Service, started filling out the seemingly endless forms to be submitted to local, state, and federal officials, began renovating the space and setting up a brewhouse, and chose a name: Ironwood Brewing. It seemed like a simple and appropriate choice. But they ran into obstacles. A woman in Valparaiso, Indiana, had converted her house into a nanobrewery and taproom and had named it after a tree in her backyard, an ironwood tree. The Michigan group had to change its chosen name and called the soon-to-open brewery Cold Iron, a reference to a particularly strong and pliable metal found deep in the earth and to a poem by Rudyard Kipling about forgiveness.

When I finally found the brewery and entered the front door, I was amazed at the size of the taproom. Nearly all of the front two-thirds of the building had been transformed into one very large space, the largest taproom I was to see in an Upper Peninsula brewery. There was a high ceiling with wood beams, and large windows around two sides made the room bright and airy. Big though it was, it seemed to be divided into separate areas: there were bar stools around the serving area, tables low and high, a lounge area, a shuffleboard area, and a small performance space. A backdoor led to a patio. "There are lots of spaces for people to do different things. We don't just want them to come here to drink beer; we want them to bring their families here for birthdays and anniversaries. We hope that there will be gatherings like weddings, anniversaries, and class reunions. Organizations can hold fund-raisers here. And we're going to have open mic nights, a mystery novels club, and trivia," John Garske told me. "We don't plan to distribute our beer; we want people to come downtown, have a pint or two, and enjoy the environment we are working hard to create."

It was in the middle of the afternoon in the middle of the week when I made my visit. Already a few people had begun to drift into the taproom. Two older men accompanied by a dog ordered beers and took a table near the window. When they sat down, Frank the Tank, the resident "brew dog," ambled over, tail wagging to greet all three. "They're regulars," Garske told me. "Every Wednesday, they come in with their dog about this time for a pint." Two grandparents and their grandchildren came in. Each of the adults enjoyed a pint, the kids a pop and some popcorn, which they shared with Frank when he came by. A couple of men, their workday over, enjoyed beers at the bar while talking with a few tourists from Nevada, who'd heard about the new brewery and had decided to come into the downtown to enjoy a flight.

"We're just getting to know our regulars and the kinds of visitors and what kinds of beer they like," Andy Warren told me. "I'm still getting used to working on a bigger system than I did when I was a home brewer, and I'm tinkering with the recipes, getting the various styles just where I'd like them to be." At the time there was a crossover blonde, an IPA, an amber ale, along with a couple of other familiar styles. And, there was something different—a gose, the tart, wheat beer whose lineage extends back centuries and to northern Germany. "It's part of my educational program," Warren said with a chuckle, "for our guests and for me. I'm pretty new at sours and I'm sure it will be something new for a lot of them. Making and drinking craft beer is an education for everyone."

When I returned to Cold Iron in 2022, I skipped the tour of Hurley's Silver Street and I didn't get lost in downtown Ironwood. But I did have trouble finding a parking spot and ended up a block or so away next to the North Country Trail. I was here specifically to chat with Andy Warren about the brewery's beers and had expected to find a quiet corner where we could sit. But there were no quiet corners. The taproom, which was filled to capacity, was the site of the party for dozens and dozens of volunteers who had worked at the annual SISU Ski-fest event held in January. It was an example of how successful Cold Iron's outreach to the community had been and how much the community had embraced the brewery. There was the happy muffled roar of conversations and the occasional outburst of laughter. Several of the guests walked over to where we were sitting to say hello to the brewer. We decided we could better conduct the interview in a storeroom behind the bar.

I asked Andy how things had changed since Cold Iron opened in 2017. "At first, we had lots of retirees; now people of all ages come in and there are more young people every year. At first our top seller was Honey Brown Cream Ale, but now it's Drift North IPA. We're getting lots of requests for Hazy IPAs, which are becoming more and more popular. And we get lots of questions, really good questions." He still gets people asking what he has that's like (name your brand) light and he has an answer: Porcupine Light. "It's 4 percent and pretty bland," he tells me, and then adds with a chuckle, "Just two-row [the base malt which provides the alcohol and water.] "He says that he mainly works making beers with subtle flavors, although "I can be bold if the style calls for it." And he loves using German hops and malts.

In describing his "six pack," Andy focused less on ingredients than on flavor. He described **Michiconsin Honey Cream** (ABV 5 percent) as not too bitter, although it does feature grapefruit notes from the Cascade hops. Corn and local honey create a smooth, rounded mouth-feel with some sweetness and the chewiness of the corn. **Mosaic Blonde** (ABV 5.2 percent), for those who want more than the basic Porcupine Light, takes its name from the hops which provide a medley of flavors from piney, to citrusy, to "bubble-gummy." It's clean, crisp, and light-bodied, with a gentle malt background.

Drift North IPA (ABV 6.9 percent) has some of the juicy tastes and hazy look of the so-called East Coast IPAs. Hops are definitely the focus, with earthy, citrus, and piney notes, while the CaraAroma malts add nutty, caramel flavors. It's a well-balanced ale, with malts and hops complementing each other. **Catherine the Great Porter** (ABV 6.5 percent) is a thick full-bodied beer dominated by coffee and chocolate flavors. In one of the brewery's videos, Andy stands outside on a winter day, taking a hearty swig of the ale. "It's a good beer for a cold day," he proclaims and, then, after draining his glass, announces, "It's a meal in a glass." **Ayer Street Amber** (ABV 6 percent) is another hearty, darker, flavorful beer. Special B malts provide caramel, burnt sugar, raisin, and biscuit flavors, while a good dose of hops contributes a flavorful balance.

And, of course, there's a blueberry beer, **Blue Collar Kolsch** (ABV 5.6 percent). This one is different. All the other UP blueberry ales I've encountered used purees bought from supply houses. This one actually uses local, hand-picked berries that are squashed down, cooked, and then added to the beer during secondary fermentation. Pink in color, the subtle blueberry taste pairs well with the delicate malt and hop flavors of the kolsch.

As we finished our discussion, a burst of applause rose from the audience in the taproom. It was for an important award being given to one of the SISU volunteers. But I thought that if the assembled group had been tasting any of the beers Andy Warren had just described, it would have been equally loud and, certainly, just as appreciative.

㉒ Five Sons Brewing Company

Five Sons Brewing Company (photo by author)

Address: 236 Main St, Marenisco, MI 49947
Phone: 906-787-2000
www.facebook.com/fivesonsbrewingmarenisco

My next stop was twenty-six miles to the east of Ironwood at a village I'd only learned about three months earlier when I discovered that a brewery had just opened there. The town, just south of Highway 2, was Marenisco. It had been a center of the logging and lumbering industries in the later nineteenth century and had been called Milltown until one of the timber magnates decided it should be renamed using the first three letters of each of the three names of his wife: Mary Enid Scott.

Marenisco is a small unincorporated community with a population of 179 according to the 2020 census. There's a gas station, convenience store, public service buildings, and the bottling plant of Superior Natural Mineral Water. There are also two bars and, since April 15, 2020, two months before my visit, Five Sons Brewing Company. The brewery was the outgrowth of the retirement hobby of Bruce and Kim Mahler. The two had long been fans of craft beer and on vacations to Germany and Austria had become interested in continental lagers. "We took a course on home brewing from Andy Warren of Cold Iron, bought a small brewing system, and soon discovered we had the most popular garage in town," Bruce remarked. When he decided to turn professional, he had the ideal location—not his garage but the small building where Kim, a medical doctor who is now retired, had established a family practice. "You're sitting in the waiting room," she told me. "The X-ray room is where the three-barrel brewhouse is." They named the business in the repurposed building after the number of their sons.

The word "community" popped up frequently during our conversation. Bruce made reference to three communities that related to his new brewery. First was the community of craft brewers. "Everyone has been so helpful. When we used to visit craft breweries, the brewers were pleased to sit down and talk with us. Bill Summers of Tribute Brewery in Eagle River, Wisconsin and Bill Reuf of Some Nerve Brewery in Manitowish Waters, Wisconsin were very helpful when we were starting up. They both came by just after we'd opened to help us celebrate." Next came the local community, both people in the village and surrounding areas, including summer residents at nearby lakes. Then, there were beer tourists who stopped at places with craft breweries. Bruce said that several of them had dropped in after they'd learned of a brewery that was scheduled to open in the spring of 2022.

"I'm making beer for people who like craft beer. I try not to get too hoppy; I want our styles to be more mellow," he said, as we began a discussion of his "six pack." **Milltown Noble Kolsch** (ABV 4.5 percent) "is what I give the locals who like the megabreweries' light beers. They like it the best of all my beers." A light-bodied, crisp, clean ale, it has a slight malty sweetness that is balanced by the spicy notes of the Tettnang hops. **Honey Ope's Honey Cream Ale** (ABV 6.6 percent), which is named after one of the Mahlers' granddaughters, uses local honey, honey malts, and flaked corn to create a creamy base whose sweetness is balanced by the floral, earthy, fruity notes of the Cluster hops.

Quail's Irish Red (ABV 5.8 percent), named after another granddaughter, is a mellow, easy-drinking version of the style. Caramel and darker roasted malts are used along with German Noble hops. **Alligator Eye PA** (ABV 5.8 percent), an English-style IPA, is "not grossly hoppy; you don't have to be a beer geek to enjoy it." Named after a rock formation on Lake Gogebic, it uses caramel, crystal, and honey malts to impart slightly sweet and caramel/toffee flavors and a medley of hops that contribute piney, grapefruit, stone fruit, and floral notes.

Kraftig Vanilla Oatmeal Stout (ABV 5.3 percent) uses roasted barley, caramel and chocolate wheat malt, along with vanilla and flaked oats to create a rich, dark, smooth ale. Northern Brewer hops provide minty, evergreen notes. **Bee Sting Honey Jalapeno Wheat** (ABV 5.3 percent) uses 50 percent wheat malt, mixes in spicy, earthy Sterling and East Kent Golding hops, honey, and wheat yeast. Then, during secondary fermentation, thirteen pounds of jalapeno peppers, which have been cut, deseeded, and frozen, are added for each two barrels of the beer. It's not too hot and offers a subtle mix of flavors.

Bruce, who was still very involved in community and civic affairs, was called away to a meeting, so Kim showed me around the building telling me what certain spaces used to be when it was her clinic, and what they are now are in Bruce's brewery. I couldn't help thinking that when people used to come through the front door, they may have wondered, "What ails me?" Now they come in wondering, "What ales will they have on tap for me?"

㉓ Alpha Michigan Brewing Company

Alpha Michigan Brewing Company
(photo courtesy Alpha Michigan Brewing Company)

Address: 303 East Center St, Alpha, MI 49902
Phone: 920-358-9551
www.alphamibeer.com
www.facebook.com/alphamibeer

Seventy-five miles east of Marenisco is another very small village that, like Marenisco, has only recently become better known because it is the home of a microbrewery. In 2018, Alpha, which by 2020 would have a population of 126 people, became the home of Alpha Michigan Brewery and proclaimed itself "the smallest village in America with a brewery." Founded in the later nineteenth century and first called Mastodon because of large prehistoric bones discovered while digging a mine shaft, the village was a center for the area's iron ore and logging activities. The name was changed to Alpha in the early twentieth century and, as the logging and then mining industries closed down, it became what it is now, a small country village around which there were some small farming and logging operations. Residents and tourists alike enjoy the area's four seasons' recreational activities.

A mile-and-a-half after the turn-off from Highway 2, a roadside sign announces: "Village of Alpha / Back Local Activities / Patronize

Local Merchants / Community Pride / Help Build Our Town." It certainly emphasizes the feeling I got when I visited: a strong sense of community togetherness. The large circle road in the center of the village seemed to link the buildings around its edge. Within the circle are held the biggest town celebrations of the year, on July 4. When I reached the brewery, which was one of the buildings around that edge, I noticed that its logo was bordered by a large green circle and in upper curve was the slogan: "Craft Brewed in the Circle." I remember having read on the brewery's website: "The Alpha Michigan Brewing Company brews with a purpose—community involvement." This includes donating a percentage of its profits to local causes and making the taproom available for fundraisers and other community events.

I sat on the patio outside the brewery and chatted with Mike Bjork, who, with Stu Creel and their wives, Mary and Julie respectively, had founded the brewery. Half-a-block away were tennis courts and a ball diamond; to the west the Porter school, built in 1914 and was the former home of specialty shops and a small café. Originally, Bjork and Creel had considered opening their brewery in the school, but, "there were just too many issues."

Mike, who had grown up in Alpha and had spent decades in the Central Intelligence Agency, had discovered "good" beer while stationed in Germany. Stu, who had bought lake property in the vicinity, had purchased a building that had been a school bus garage and turned it into a grocery store, complete with a walk-in cooler. Mike had returned home, the husbands and wives became friends, and they decided to transform the grocery store into a brewery and taproom. "We were neophytes; neither of us had ever brewed. We wanted to have fun and do something for the community."

"We had no idea we'd be so successful," Mike commented. "We got good coverage from the TV stations and from word of mouth. We get people from the area, vacationers camping in the lakes around here, a people passing through. We've got seventy more members in our mug club than there are people living in the village." The popularity of the brewery was really evident during the 2019 Fourth of July celebrations. They ran out of beer and the "calamity" even made it into the evening news.

During our conversation, Mike occasionally went inside to talk with Lydia Novitsky, who was working on a batch of beer. A

Detroit native who had moved to the UP, she'd seen an ad asking for help in the brewhouse. "It said, 'No Experience Necessary'," she told me a few minutes later. "I was tired of my other job, I liked craft beer, and I would be exciting to learn something new." She joined Mike and Stu as the brewers, replacing Mary Bjork, who had handled some of the brewing duties in Alpha's early years. In the fall, she would become the lead brewer.

"We offer a broad range of craft beer styles," Mike said. "The people who come in enjoy variety. And we try to use local ingredients as often as possible. We've used local hops and for our fruit beers, we don't use extracts. We've used rhubarb and we pick the wild blueberries. It's a community effort. We even have a zesting team of customers come in to help us zest oranges when we are doing a wheat beer"

The first three beers Mike chose for his "six pack," many of which had local names, were fairly strong beers: 6.7 percent ABV and above. **Brule River Red** (ABV 6.7 percent) is an American-style amber ale which balances the sweetness of the caramel malts with the grapefruity tartness of the Cascade hops. **Porter School Porter** (ABV 6. 7 percent) is a dark, rich, full-bodied beer with a slightly burnt taste. Local maple syrup gives an added richness. A medley of hops provides spicy, apple, pepper, and earthy flavors that moderate the sweetness. **Bear's Cave IPA** (ABV 7.1 percent) is definitely a hop-forward West Coast version of the style. Centennial and Chinook hops contribute bitterness and strong citrus and grapefruit notes, while crystal and Munich malts add caramel and toasted flavors. Mike noted that the beer used local hops and grains when they were available.

Naughty School Girl Cream Ale (ABV 5.9 percent) is described in the beer menu as a "lawnmower" beer, although it's stronger than most crossover beers. It's lightly hopped. Flaked corn and honey malts give a smooth, rich texture. **Blueberry Muffin Wheat Beer** (ABV 5.2 percent) uses local blueberries. **Book Mine Brown Ale** (ABV 4.6 percent) has chocolate, caramel, nutty, and toasty flavors that are complemented with a hop spiciness.

Lydia excused herself to check on things in the brewhouse. "We've got a lot of beer to make in the next couple of weeks," Mike said. "Fourth of July is coming up." Running out three years earlier had been quite an event and good publicity. But to run out again ...?

㉔ 51ˢᵗ State Brewing Company

51st State Brewing Company(photo by author)

Address: 115 Harding Ave, Kingsford, MI 49802
Phone: 906-828-2167,
www.51ststatebrewingco.com,
www.facebook.com/51stStateBrewingCo

With a combined population of 12,491, the twin cities of Iron Mountain-Kingsford, located 30 miles east of Alpha, is the largest "metropolitan area" on the Michigan stretch of Highway 2. (Escanaba is second, with 311 fewer people.) Iron Mountain had been a major mining center from the later nineteenth century to the early 1930s, while Kingsford had been a home to a Ford Motor plant from the early 1920s to the early 1950s. It was also the place where charcoal briquettes, that popular fuel among beer-drinking outdoor cooks, had been invented. From 1891 to the onset of Prohibition, the Upper Michigan (also called Upper Peninsula) Brewing Company had created beverages to slake the thirsts of miners and others.

51ˢᵗ State Brewing(the name is a reference to a one-time move-ment to declare the Upper Peninsula and parts of northern

Wisconsin a separate state), the first brewery in the area in nearly a century, is located at the edge of a residential district in Kingsford. When I first visited in 2017, the building renovations were nearly complete and the often painfully slow permitting processes well underway. Jeff Brickey, head brewer and co-owner with his wife, Victoria, was connecting parts of the brewhouse together in preparation for the scheduled early 2018 opening. Why, I asked him, did he decide to locate his brewery so far away from Highway 2, which passes through the main part of Ironwood? "We wanted to be off the beaten path," he told me. "We're in a community with houses, apartments, even an assisted living facility. People will be able to walk or bicycle here. Passersby have told me that they plan to bring relatives from the assisted living facility here in their wheelchairs. We won't be a bar; we'll be a brewery that makes its own food. Families will be welcome—parents, grandparents, and kids."

I also asked him why a retired plant manager of a Marinette, Wisconsin foundry, who'd moved to his wife's hometown of Marquette, had decided to turn his home brewing hobby into a profession. "I'd done the travel thing; motor home tours and cruises. I was bored and wanted to take my home brewing hobby to a new level. I wanted to keep learning and to have new challenges." He looked at a few towns in the UP and settled on Kingsford. "It was large enough to support a small brewery and there weren't any craft breweries nearby. The Kingsford and Iron Mountain communities were very welcoming."

When I visited again in 2022, I asked Brickey if his plans for the brewery had met his expectations. "More than met!" he exclaimed. "I reached my five-year goals after two." He'd had some educating to do. "In Marquette, there were a lot of experienced beer drinkers. Vierling had opened in the mid-nineties and later Blackrocks and Ore Dock. People were familiar with a wide range of styles. A smoked beer would go well over there, but not here. People weren't ready for something like a Belgian Tripel or a Double Bock." What he did discover was that people were ready for fruit beers. He made a blueberry ale, thinking it might appeal to craft beer novices and, he added, to women who really didn't like beer. "But it exploded. It's by far our best seller; people get upset when they come in and discover we're out of it."

The other big surprise was the success of their decision to create a pizza menu. "The people from the Michigan Brewers Guild suggested that having food would prevent people from just having a beer and then going somewhere else to eat. Victoria has made all sorts of specialty pizzas. Sometimes we sell over one hundred in a day. There's a big Italian population in the area and our pizzas have been named the best in Iron Mountain/Kingsford." Some of the specialty pizzas advertised on the brewery's Facebook page are Pizza of the Gods (tarragon-citrus sauce), Big Dill Pizza with bacon, and Pulled Pork with roasted sweet corn.

The beers in Jeff's "six pack" all carry nicknames that link them to area landmarks or history. **Batty Millie Blueberry Wheat** (ABV 5.4 percent) is named after an abandoned mine shaft that has now become home for thousands and thousands of bats. The ale is a smooth-bodied, rich and creamy beverage with strong blueberry and vanilla flavors. Amarillo hops provide balancing stone fruit and citrus notes. **Ski Jump IPA** (ABV 7.6 percent), a tribute to the world-class sports venue in Iron Mountain, has piney, stone fruit, and citrus flavors against a strong malt background. **State of Superior Pale Ale** (ABV 7 percent), a reference to the name a hypothetical 51st state might have, is a typical American version of the style. Easy-drinking in spite of its high alcohol percentage, it has little malt background. The hops provide the dominant earthy, herbal, grapefruit flavors.

GC-RA Glider American Porter (ABV 5.3) is named after the famous World War II flying machine that was manufactured in Kingsford. The ale is noted for its rich medley of flavors which include coffee, molasses, and stone fruit. **3 Vagabonds American Pilsner** (ABV 5.8 percent) is a transition beer which uses pilsner malts and Saaz hops to give a light-bodied lager reminiscent of the German versions of the style. "The Three Vagabonds" is the name Henry Ford, Harvey Firestone, and Thomas Edison gave themselves on their wandering camping trips through the Upper Peninsula. **On Island Time Hazy IPA** (ABV 8 percent) is a New England style IPA dominated by such tropical fruit flavors as mango.

"I thought about and visited a lot of different places before settling here," Brickey said. "I made the right choice. The people here really like our beer and our pizzas, and I really like being part of this neighborhood."

<table>
<tr><td>**Ale Trail**
8</td><td>## Menominee, Escanaba,
Cooks, Manistique</td></tr>
</table>

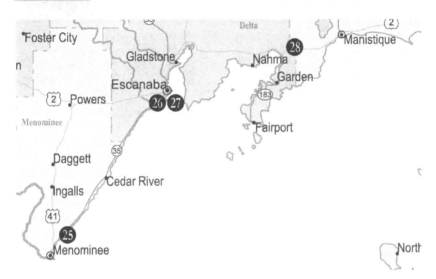

The cities along the northern shore of Lake Michigan have a long brewing history. Between 1870 and 1961, Menominee hosted three breweries. Two operated in Escanaba between 1874 and 1940, and one in Manistique between 1903 and 1909. Each of these cities was located at the mouth of one of the Upper Peninsula's great logging rivers and was the home of one or more sawmills, and each had a large enough population to support a brewery. However, after the Menominee-Marinette Brewing Company plant closed in 1961, locally brewed beer did not return to the northern shores of Lake Michigan until 1994, when Hereford & Hops, located in a historic building in downtown Escanaba, became the Upper Peninsula's first craft brewery and brewpub. By early 2023, there would be five breweries between Menominee and Manistique. They ranged in size from small family operations to a large production brewery that had recently been purchased by the subsidiary of an international corporation.

㉕ Three Bridge Brewing Company

Three Bridge Brewing Company(photo by author)

Address: 2221 Thirteenth St, Menominee, MI 49858
Phone: 906-399-9611,
www.facebook.com/threebridgebrewing

I began the final leg of my Upper Peninsula Circ-Ale tour a mile north of the Interstate Bridge that connects Wisconsin and Michigan. Turning off Highway 41, I crossed the railroad tracks and parked in front of a small building that had originally been a real estate office but had stood empty before being transformed into the brewery and taproom of Three Bridge Brewing Company, which opened in 2018. I was early for my interview, and the owners/brewers Kris and Sarah Rusch had not yet arrived. It turned out that they'd made a trip to a nearby farm to donate their spent grains to be used as pig feed. "It's recycling," Kris later told me. "The spent grains help create the meat that we enjoy eating with one of our beers."

I took a short stroll around the neighborhood. The houses were old and some of them had been converted into small businesses. One was a beauty salon and another was a gourmet hot dog restaurant, "Yooper Dogz," Kris and Sarah arrived as I was leaving Yooper Dogz and invited me into the taproom. It was small, a few bar stools and tables and a door leading to a little beer garden with four picnic tables. Relatively simple and plain, with the exception of a mural above the bar that had been painted by a local artist, it had no television set, and the thick cinder block walls made it impervious to cell phone reception. "People can't look at their phones or stare at the TV. They enjoy talking with each other," Kris told me.

A native of Escanaba, Kris had earned a masters degree in Experimental Psychology at Northern Michigan University, with a thesis that involved, according to his LinkedIn page, "behavioral pharmacology with rodents." He became disenchanted with the politics of the profession and, alarmed by the chemicals that were being used in the experiments, decided it was time for a career change. "I'd been a home brewer and I liked craft brews. Bell's Two Hearted Ale showed me the wonderful things hops could do, and Founder's Dirty Bastard Scotch, what malts could do. Beer was a drug I liked. It was a social lubricant and it was a lot safer than the chemicals I was giving to the rodents." He decided to enroll in the Ashville-Buncombe Technical Community College in the Brewing and Distilling Program, earned an associate degree, worked for several months in an area brewery and returned to Michigan to pursue a dream: "I always knew I wanted to start my own brewery."

He had a partner in his quest, his now-wife Sarah, who was from the Milwaukee area and who, by her own admission, "didn't know much about beer. Kris was my teacher." The two of them are the co-owners and only paid employees. They did most of the grunt work of turning the abandoned building into a taproom and brewhouse. "We had help from our friends—unpaid labor. They even helped us test our beer recipes as we developed them."

Kris chose Menominee as the site for his new brewery. And he shares why: "There were other places I might have chosen, but this seemed the right one. There was no brewery in town; the area was economically depressed and a brewery could be one of the catalysts in a revival. People were accepting of me: I'm a Yooper and like so many people around here I love the outdoors. Moreover I'm a political moderate—I'm not going to alienate anyone."

But there were challenges and roadblocks. The first involved a city ordinance that prohibited the sale of liquor at a place closer than five hundred feet from the nearest residential dwelling. There was a house just behind the proposed brewery. "The community rallied around us, and we got past that problem." Then there was a matter of a name. Rusch, who was an admirer of the ancient Greek philosopher Plato, had wanted to call his brewery "Wise Man," a nod to the philosopher's supposed statement: "It was a wise man who invented beer." But that was taken. Then he considered the name "Three Bridges" a reference to both Plato's discussion of the three bridges connecting the mythical kingdom of Atlantis and to the fact that Menominee was connected to its sister city Marinette, Wisconsin, by three bridges. But that, too, was taken. So, he lopped the "s" off of "bridges" and had a name that reflected both the city and his interest in Greek philosophy.

Since opening, Three Bridge has offered a wide variety of beers ranging from German lagers to what Rusch calls "dessert beers," which include different fruits and which, he says, "we do just for fun." Two of his year-around beers, Sky Kettle Marzen and Stuttgart Helles, reflect the influence of the German tradition on his brewing. "I am of German heritage," he emphasizes. They are not only favorites of the growing number of aficionados of classic German lager styles, but also offer people used to the bland pale American lagers of the mega brewers a tasty, non-threatening introduction to craft beers. Medium-to-light-bodied, the malts in **Sky Kettle Marzen** (ABV 5 percent) contribute bready, slightly-sweet flavors complemented by the mild spiciness of the Nugget and Tettnang hops. **Stuttgart Helles** (ABV 4.7 percent) is fuller-bodied than pilsners or mass market American lagers. A touch of sweet maltiness is balanced by the tang of the Noble hops.

Three Bridge has offered a variety of IPAs: East Coast, West Coast, Imperial. "I like to highlight the characteristics of a single hop in our IPAs," Rusch says. **Excursion Zone** (ABV 6.6 percent), for example, uses Mosaic hops, which offer tropical fruit and citrus notes. **Dreamwalker** (ABV 7.1 percent) is what has become known as a milkshake IPA, a fuller-bodied ale in which vanilla and orange concentrate and milk sugar are added to a base IPA.

Other frequently available beers include **Barbarian**, a Schwarz-bier. "It's a porter-like beer," Kris explains. "It's lighter, but the chocolate malts provide a relaxed but robust drinking experience." **BenoFino** (ABV 5.4 percent) is a brown ale that uses coffee beans ground locally and maple syrup from a nearby farm. **Belly Warmer**

Old Fashioned Winter Ale (ABV 6.7 percent) adds cherry concentrate and orange rind to a Sky Kettle Marzen base to create a drink that is like an "Old Fashioned" cocktail, one of the very popular mixed drinks in the Upper Peninsula. **Lovely Lady Pina Colada** (ABV 4.6 percent), a dessert beer, has subtle hints of pineapple and coconut which play against the helles base with its Nugget and Tettnang hops.

Three Bridge Brewing opened in the fall of 2018 with a one-barrel brewing system. "Because it was small, we were able to try out a lot of different recipes," Kris remembered, "but it meant we had to brew every day or run out. So we graduated to a two-barrel system and then to a seven. We'd like to expand again so that we can distribute our beer locally and around the UP and northern Wisconsin."

㉖ Upper Hand Brewery

Upper Hand Brewery (photo by author)

Address: 3525 Airport Rd, Escanaba, MI 49829
Phone: 906-233-5005,
www.upperhandbrewery.com,
www.facebook.com/UpperHandBrewery

Michigan Highway 35, which connects Menominee with Escanaba, runs for fifty-five miles along the shores of Lake Michigan (or, to be more specific, the western shores of Green Bay). There are stretches of open beach, many summer homes, campgrounds, and a handful of boat launch sites. There are also several miles where the road on both sides is bounded by second and third growth forests, the descendants of the great pines and hardwoods cut during the late nineteenth century logging era. Upper Hand Brewery, one of the three large production breweries in the UP, is located just south of Escanaba.

In 2012, I'd heard rumors that Larry Bell, the founder of Bell's Brewery, one of the largest craft breweries in the country, was going to start a brewery in Escanaba. He had family connections with the Upper Peninsula that extended back to the early twentieth century and had summer homes in Gulliver and Curtis. It had long been a dream of his to open a brewery in the UP. He considered operating in Marquette and Manistique, but by late 2012 had settled on Escanaba and had begun meetings with the Escanaba City Council and Chamber of Commerce. By mid-2013, he'd purchased property in the Delta County Renaissance Zone, near Delta County Airport, and a year later, Upper Hand Brewery was in full operation.

At first, many people assumed that the new brewery would be "Bell's North," a second production plant that would make such well-known beers as Two Hearted Ale and Oberon Wheat Ale and distribute them through the upper Midwest. But in newspaper articles, Bell stated that he wanted to create a brand that would fit the Upper Peninsula, This became immediately apparent from the name he chose for his new venture: Upper Hand Brewery. Looked at a certain way, the Upper Peninsula looks like the silhouette of a hand, with the index finger pointing toward Sault Ste Marie, and the Keweenaw Peninsula jutting into Lake Superior like a thumb. The name distinguished the location of his brewery from the Lower Peninsula, often called "The Mitten."

When I made my first visit to Upper Hand in 2017, I was greeted by Sam Reese, then the Production Manager. He'd become a home brewer shortly after he'd entered Western Michigan University in Kalamazoo, "right in Bell's back yard," as he put it. He worked after graduation for Abita Brewing, Louisiana's largest craft brewer, before returning to Kalamazoo, where he was hired on at Bell's and began working his way up the production ladder. He'd been in charge of operations in Escanaba since Upper Hand had opened.

We discussed the philosophy and branding of Upper Hand. "Larry wanted a brand independent from Bell's, with different kinds of beer, something special for the UP," Sam explained. He noted that, although some Upper Hand product is distributed to northern Wisconsin and Minnesota, most is sold in the Upper Peninsula. "We wanted to establish a solid UP footprint; at first, we decided not to sell any of our beer below the bridge." The names of the early beers offered for sale emphasized local identity: Escanaba Black Beer (discontinued in 2022), Yooper Ale, and 906 Ale (a reference to the UP area code). In developing beer recipes, they wanted beers that were approachable and sessionable. "Up here, people like to drink beer while doing other things they enjoy—camping, boating, skiing, fishing, working around the yard or at the cabin, so we didn't want our core list to be too high in alcoholic content."

When I revisited Upper Hand in June 2022, several things had changed. The brewery was still located beside the airport and was hidden from the highway by a stand of trees. I was again greeted by Sam Reese, but he had been promoted from Production to Operations Director. The brewery had been expanded and annual production more than doubled; cans had replaced bottles. The product was now distributed throughout Michigan, but was no longer available in nearby states. Most important, the company had been sold. In late 2021, Larry Bell announced that he had sold Bell's (and its subsidiary, Upper Hand) to New Belgium Brewing, one of the United States' largest craft breweries. New Belgium, itself, had been sold in 2019 to Lion Little World Beverage of Australia, itself a subsidiary of Kirin, an international beverage conglomerate operating out of Japan.

Sam gave me a tour through the expanded brewery. We stopped to watch as workers stacked flats of just-canned UPA (Upper Peninsula Ale) on pallets. "A lot of this will be going south of the Mackinac Bridge," he told me. The tour over, we retired to the taproom/gift shop, where we were joined by marketing specialist Dannielle Tankersley. The taproom had been an afterthought. "We began as a production brewery only," Sam told me. "But so many people kept showing up at our door wanting to buy beer and souvenirs that we had to build one. Most of them were tourists from out of state or the Lower Peninsula and they wanted to bring back some UP beer and maybe a hat or glass as a memento of their trip to the Upper Peninsula."

Sam recalled his time working for Abita in Louisiana. "Their beer was available in other states, but it came out of a specific cultural climate. We have worked on doing the same kind of thing here. We set out to make beers that would evoke a sense of the UP: the people, the places, and the activities." He paused, chuckled, and then added: "Even the mosquitoes." He was referring to State Bird Blood Orange Saison IPA. The idea of blood orange recalled mosquitoes' favorite diet. The label pictured two very large mosquitoes perched on a highway marker that read "State Bird." Other names also evoked the Upper Peninsula: Laughing Fish (an echo of Laughing Whitefish River), Yooper, Deer Camp, Sisu (the Finnish term for determination and grit). Labels pictured, among other things, campfires, fishermen, a small town, the Mackinac Bridge, a maple sugar shack, a car stuck in the snow, and lighthouses. The website proudly stated that the beers were "brewed by a crew of hikers, bikers, campers, dog-walkers, anglers, hunters and outdoor loving Yoopers."

Of course, the important thing was the beer in the cans with the UP images and names. "We work to make our beers consistently good and approachable," Sam noted. I remarked that I'd noticed that nine of the twenty beers described on the website were below 5 percent ABV and that only five were above 7 percent. The beers were intended to be enjoyed by active people, to be session beers sipped during a break during or after outdoor activities. Three of the stronger beers were an IPA, a wild berry sour, and the Sisu Stout, a hefty 10 percent—definitely an after-activity beverage.

When I asked Sam and Dannielle to select a "six pack" of Upper Hand beers and describe them to me, their first three choices were three lighter beers designed to appeal both to drinkers new to craft beer and veterans. **Yooper Ale** (ABV 4 percent), available only in the Upper Peninsula, is an American session pale ale. Light-bodied and easy to drink, it has "tons" of Citra and Cascade hops that give both citrus and piney flavors, along with Upper Peninsula grown oats, which not only create a haziness, but also add a creamy texture and a nutty flavor. **Upper Hand Light** (ABV 4.2 percent) was created because, as Sam noted, "You need a light lager in the UP." When he said that, I remember that Busch Light was the biggest selling beer in the UP. Pilsner and Carapils malts give a malty base while the Noble hops add a spiciness. **Laughing Fish Ale** (ABV 4.9 percent), described on the can as a "Northern Golden Ale," is based on German kolsch. Vienna malts provide a gentle malt base, while Glacier hops give a lemony tang. Clean and crisp, it is definitely a mid-afternoon thirst quencher.

The second group of beers ranged in strength from 4.7 ABV to 7.0. **Deer Camp Amber Lager** (ABV 4.7 percent) is an enormously popular seasonal release which appears on the market just before the most popular season for a very large part of the UP population: mid-to- late-fall deer hunting season. It's an Oktoberfest style beer that, Sam noted, tastes like Yuengling's Lager, an extremely popular lager from Pennsylvania. "It only comes in twelve-packs," Dannielle remarked. "Nobody takes a six pack to deer camp." And it's low enough in alcohol that if you have more than one, you're probably not going to get into trouble. **UPA—Upper Peninsula Ale** (ABV 5.5) is the first beer Upper Hand released in 2014 and still a big seller. It's referred to as an "old-school pale ale," a style that had been around before Sierra Nevada created their now famous version of the style. UPA begins with a malty, nutty flavor and ends with a gentle hop finish that mixes piney, citrus, and floral notes. The crystal malts also add a slight sweetness. **Upper Hand IPA** (ABV 7.0 percent)—there is no nickname although fifteen were considered and discarded—is designed to be a balanced and approachable version of the style. Medium-bodied, it has less of the hop assertiveness of West Coast American IPAs and a little more of the malty earthiness and sweetness associated with English IPAs. Amarillo and Crystal hops add floral, fruity, and piney characteristics generally found in West Coast IPAs.

"Whether someone is enjoying an Upper Hand beer in the Upper Peninsula or somewhere else, we want them to look at the illustrations on the can, take a big sip and think about this wonderful part of Michigan." I did. Later that afternoon, I sat on my dock enjoying a Laughing Fish, and then saved some Upper Hand beers to take back with me to enjoy a few weeks later as I sat under the backyard pergola of my home in the high desert of New Mexico. I knew that when I did that, I'd happily think of Michigan's Upper Hand: the Upper Peninsula.

㉗ Hereford & Hops Steakhouse and Brewpub

Hereford & Hops Steakhouse and Brewpub (photo by author)

Address: 624 Ludington St, Escanaba, MI 49829
Phone: 906-789-1945,
www.herefordandhops.com
www.facebook.com/HerefordandHops

It was a ten-minute drive along M-35—past the end of the airport runway, the Escanaba golf course, the public and Catholic high schools to Ludington Avenue, Escanaba's main street, and then east along Ludington—to the next stop on this ale trail: a building of double historical importance. Built in 1914 as a luxury hotel, the Delta Hotel is on the National Register of Historic Places and is home to Hereford & Hops Steakhouse and Brewpub, the Upper Peninsula's first craft brewery. Since the late 1990s, I'd been enjoying lunch here during my annual day trips to the city known as the center of the UP's "banana belt." On one of my visits, I'd sampled my first Upper Peninsula version of kolsch, a German-style beer that was relatively unknown across the United States at that time, but has since become very popular among craft beer drinkers.

I first met the owner of Hereford & Hops, the late Don Moody, in 2017, when I'd arrived to do an interview with brewer Mike Sattem. Mike was brewing and while we were waiting, Don showed me around the brewpub, which occupies most of the first floor of the building (the upper floors house apartments). At the front was the seven-barrel brewhouse, visible behind the floor-to-ceiling plate glass panels that formed one of the walls beside an elegant, full-service bar. Next to the bar was a cozy pub area that had a pool table, oversized easy chairs and a sofa, a gas fireplace, and, above it, one of the establishment's four TVs. A formal dining room, featuring tables set with white cloths and a fully-restored player grand piano, was behind the pub area, and, next to it, a large grill where patrons could cook their own steaks. Past the grill was a room nicknamed "The Other Grill," a Mongolian grill where patrons filled bowls with ingredients that would be handed to a chef to be grilled.

Many years ago, Don, a native of Kankakee, Illinois, and his wife and young family used to spend summers in Rock, a small community north of Escanaba. "We had a small farm. I decided to raise Hereford cattle at the farm, and we moved to the UP permanently." He and a neighbor purchased the Delta Hotel building and, when, in 1992, the Michigan Government changed its liquor laws to allow brewpubs, they decided to build one. He also took a crash course in brewing. In the months after the December 1994 opening, the idea of grilling your own steak and drinking beer brewed on premises became so popular that there were lineups of people waiting to get in: locals, day-trippers from as far away as Marquette and Green Bay, and, in the summer, tourists, including an increasing number of beer tourists.

One of the people who had worked on the renovations of the Delta Hotel in the early 1990 was Mike Sattem, a recent high school graduate. "I never thought it would happen," he said as he joined Don Mooney and me in the dining room. "Now here we are, twenty-five years later, two people who'd had no experience brewing, an owner and a head brewer." After Hereford & Hops had opened, Mike began hanging around John Malchow, who'd taken over from Moody as the brewer, picking up as much information he could about the brewing process. He apprenticed in the brewery of a sister restaurant in Wausau, Wisconsin and was part of the brewing team that won three World Beer Cup and two Great

American Beer Festival medals. When Malchow moved on, Mike returned to Escanaba and has been there since, making him, along with Derek "Chumley" Anderson of Vierling Restaurant and Marquette Harbor Brewery and Lark Ludlow of Tahquamenon Falls Brewery, the longest-serving brewers in the UP.

When I met Mike Sattem again in 2022, the beer list included many of the styles I recognized from my earlier visits. There had been some changes, Mike noted. He now often brewed lesser-known styles, including the growingly popular sour beers, which he said he stored in a different part of the brewery's basement to prevent any contamination. He also has lowered the alcohol percentage of most of the beers as patrons' tastes evolved. "Most people enjoy something that complements their food, not something over the top." But he also noted that as people's familiarity with craft beers evolved, they were more accepting of hoppy beers.

"When we started out, we developed Whitetail as a gentle beer, but people thought it was too hoppy." **Whitetail Golden Ale** (ABV 4.7 percent) is one of Hereford & Hops' flagship beers. A gold medal winner at the World Beer Cup, it has a light-to-medium malt body and a crisp hop finish that has earthy, pine, and citrus notes. Another beer designed for novice drinkers of craft beer is the very low ABV **Bluegrass Wheat Ale** (ABV 3.1 percent), a blueberry-flavored ale which uses lemongrass instead of hops. This unusual ingredient provides ginger and lemon flavors that balance the fairly unassertive two-row barley and wheat malts and complement the hint of blueberries.

Cleary Irish Red Ale (ABV 4.8 percent), winner of a Great American Beer Festival bronze medal, and **Blackbird Oatmeal Stout** (ABV 6.1 percent), winner of a World Beer Cup bronze, are two of Hereford & Hops darker brews. **Cleary Red** is a medium-bodied amber given a malty sweetness by the caramel malts and touch of candy apple-flavoring. The stout is a medium- to full-bodied version of the style given a silky, creamy texture by the oats, and roasted and coffee notes by the dark malts. **Redemption IPA** originally started at 5.5 percent ABV, but, Sattem told me, "I gradually ramped up the ABV to 7.5 percent as people's palates developed. Medium-to full-bodied, it has an array of hops, including Simcoe, Cascade, and Amarillo, that contribute citrus, earthy, piney, spicy, and floral notes to complement the malty backbone. The **Kolsch** (no ABV available) is light-bodied, crisp, and clean-finishing. It follows the German recipe as closely as possible and is a refreshing, almost lager-like drink.

I'd visited the brewhouse on my previous trip, but asked Mike if we could tour it again. "I've just finished cleaning everything, including the windows. People are much more worried," he added, "if all the equipment isn't clean, the beer will be no good." Between the mash tun and brew kettle hung a sign that I remembered from my earlier visit. "Blessed is the mother who gives birth to a brewer." Mike laughed and told me that, although his mother is proud of him, she doesn't drink any alcohol. I remarked that I was sure that many, many of the people who had enjoyed his beer had probably blessed her.

㉘ LaTulip Brewing Company

LaTulip Brewing Company (photo by author)

Address: 11858W US Highway 2, Cooks, MI 49817
Phone: 906-644-2317
www.facebook.com/latulipbrewingco

Although the first craft brewery in the Upper Peninsula was established in Escanaba in 1994, the 143-mile stretch along Highway 2 from Escanaba to St. Ignace along the shores of Lake Michigan was a figurative "craft beer desert" until the summer of 2022. Mackinaw Trail Winery and Brewery had opened in Manistique in 2015, but relocated to Petoskey, a forty- minute drive south of the Mackinac Bridge, in early 2018. Then in August of 2022, LaTulip Brewing opened in Cooks, a community thirteen miles west of Manistique and, in the spring of 2023, Flatiron Brewing was scheduled to begin operations just south of Manistique near the banks of the Manistique River.

I first heard of LaTulip Brewing in the spring of 2021 when neighbors at the lake, knowing of my interest in breweries, told me of a large billboard on US Highway 2 announcing that a brewery would be opening soon in a nearby building that had most recently housed a winery, Yooper Wines. There was no one there when I stopped and peered into the windows, but there was evidence of extensive renovations going on. A few weeks later when I passed by, there was a pickup truck in the parking lot. I knocked on the door and was greeted by Jason LaTulip, who, with his cousin, Jeff, was well into the long and sometimes frustrating process of opening a brewery. The seven-barrel brewing system had arrived, the taproom was taking shape, and a fence was being built around a large outside area that would serve as a beer garden. Jason and Jeff had begun the long process in November of 2020 and had originally hoped to open for business in 2021. However, when I visited, the hoped-for date had been moved to the summer of 2022.

In June 2022, I visited Jeff, who had moved with his wife, Alecia, three children and two dogs into a large fifth-wheel parked behind the brewery. "Things are just about ready to go," he told me. "We have some finishing touches for the building, some more inspections, and permitting, and then we're ready to go." They already had four tanks filled with beer that they couldn't sell until all the paperwork was finally completed.

"It wasn't until I went to school at Michigan Tech in Houghton and visited Keweenaw Brewing's taproom that I discovered what beer could be. I got hooked on craft beer and began making my own. I'd been brewing for seven years when Alecia and I decided we wanted to become proprietors. Starting a brewery seemed like a good idea. After we'd incorporated and bought the building, the learning process began." Jason and Jeff went to Colorado where they took an intensive three-day course with Tom Hennessey, a legendary craft brewing pioneer who once produced a video called "Frankenbrew," about creating a brewhouse out of used materials including dairy tanks. "It was one-on-one-brewing, the business side of operations, customer service. Then we did a batch of beer at Colorado's Big Choice Brewery, which had the same kind of system as we did."

While renovating the building, setting up the brewhouse, filling out the forms, and often simply waiting, Jeff was developing recipes. "We hope to have two or three 'normal' beers, such as a golden ale, light lager, and amber that new craft beer drinkers will enjoy." There will be darker beers: stout, porter, and brown ales, English IPAs, and some things that might be considered what Jeff called "way out:" a farmhouse ale with yeast sourced near his mother's garden, and a cucumber sour beer.

Late in August, when the final approvals had been granted and LaTulip Brewing at last opened, seven beers were on the menu. There were two "normal beers," **Light Lager** (ABV 4 percent) and **Blonde Ale** (ABV 4.5 percent). The former had a gentle malt flavor with an understated hop spiciness. Light-bodied and smooth, it was a good introduction to craft beer. The latter was light-to-medium-bodied with a creamy, smooth mouth-feel with a crisp hop finish. The **Irish Red Ale** (4.7 percent ABV) was a maltier, slightly sweet, medium-bodied ale, while the **IPA**(ABV 5.8 per cent) had the earthiness and more understated hop presence of English interpretations of the style. The **Stout** (ABV 5 percent) was smooth, chocolatey and mellow, medium-bodied and very drinkable. **Farmhouse Saison** (ABV 6.4 percent) was an easy-drinking, slightly peppery version of the old European ale. **Cucumber Sour** (ABV 4.5 percent) turned the unlikely combination of ingredients into a refreshing summer beer, slightly bitter and crisp.

㉙ Flatiron Brewing Company

Flatiron Brewing Company
(photo courtesy Flat Iron Brewing Company)

Address: 375 Traders Point Dr Stop #4; Manistique, MI 49854
Phone: 616-500-3808
www.flatiron-brewing.com; www.facebook.com/FlatironBrewing

In mid-fall 2021, a few weeks after my first visit to LaTulip Brewing, I learned that a new brewery was planned for Manistique. Flatiron Brewing was to be located in Traders Point, south of Highway 2 and a few dozen yards from the western shore of the Manistique River. The area had become popular in recent years as a destination for locals and tourists, with a restaurant, gift shop, outdoor recreation rental shop, and campground. It is also the site of "Hops on the Harbor," an annual beer festival held in August.

The website described the owners as "individuals with a passion for beer [and] a love of Manistique who wanted to give back to the community." Over the next year or so, I'd enjoyed reading about the progress of the brewery: the creating of trial brews, the hiring of a consultant to develop a menu of pizza, salads, appetizers, and desserts. Also posted were pictures of dining equipment and brewing apparatus and of the special mugs being created for charter members of the Mug Club. When I spoke to one of the owners, he remarked that there would be a very large taproom, with room for a pool table, dart board, and a performance space. This would not just be a place for beer and pizza, but a place for community members and tourists to meet and gather.

I'm looking forward to visiting Flatiron Brewing after it opens in the spring of 2023. I'll try to make it my final stop on the long, four-day journey from Albuquerque to the little cabin in the big woods. That way I'll be able to pick up a new brew for my celebratory first sip on the dock of the bay.

Last Call

It was an early autumn evening at the lake. The day had been gray and drizzly. Late in the afternoon, a brisk north wind had blown up, lowering the temperatures and churning up the lake. It was no day to sip on the dock, and so, dinner over, I lit a fire and alternately watched the whitecaps racing to the south and the flames dancing in the fireplace. I sipped a pint of Blackrocks' Cockney Mild, an English dark mild that's one of my favorite autumn beers. Dark, full-bodied and rich, it seemed the appropriate beer to celebrate the end of the summer season. The sun broke through the clouds, touching the whitecaps and then sank behind the birches, maples, and poplars that had already begun to turn golden and scarlet.

I put another log on the fire and thought about the journey of a thousand sips I'd begun nearly four months ago. I had traveled across most of the Upper Peninsula, beside the shores of three great lakes, through forests and across many rivers, and into villages, towns, and cities. I visited twenty-nine craft breweries and taprooms (one of which would close in the early autumn), some in buildings that were well over a century old, others that were in the repurposed homes of former businesses, and a couple that had been built specifically to house breweries. (I even peered through the windows of two buildings that were being converted into breweries that would be opening in the winter.) And in these buildings I met brewers and owners (many of the people being both) and listened as they talked about the beers they loved to create and to share with people who visited their taprooms and brewpubs.

Many people who, in the early spring, had learned of my proposed journey had said, a note of envy in their voices, that it must be fun to drive around all day, visiting breweries, and drinking beer. It was fun to drive and visit, but the sips were few and far between. I'd occasionally have a small glass of something unusual a brewer had just made, but mostly I depended on the generosity of the brewers who would gift me with a growler or crowler or a six-pack or two as our visit ended. These I would enjoy and take notes about when I returned to the cabin and sipped on the dock of the bay.

And what a wonderful variety of beers there were. Of course, there were the staples of the craft beer movement, such as India pale ales, wheat beers, stouts, and many versions of the Upper Peninsula's "national beer," blueberry ale. But there were several beers that I wouldn't have seen if I'd made my journey a decade or so earlier: German goses, Berliner weisses, Alt biers; Franco-Belgian saisons, and Mexican lagers. There was even a resurgence of pale American lagers, which craft brewers had eschewed making until a few years ago.

What most impressed me as I traveled the ale trails of the Upper Peninsula was how very local each craft brewery or brewpub was. The owners and brewers were part of the communities: some had been born and raised in the towns where they established breweries; several had left the area but had returned, often with the specific goal of opening a brewery; a few had moved to the Upper Peninsula many years earlier because their spouses had come from there. Only one brewery, Upper Hand Brewery, was not local. Originally created by Larry Bell, the founder of Kalamazoo's Bell's Brewery, it had been acquired by an international network of brewing companies under the control of Kirin of Japan. But when I visited, I found that most of the people who worked in the Escanaba plant were local and that the brews created there reinforced the cultural link between the company and the community.

It's difficult to predict how many more breweries can be created in the Upper Peninsula. One brewer told me that if prospective brewery owners had a sound business plan and solid financing and could find a receptive market, they stood a good chance of success. "But," he emphasized, "they have to make good beer. The Upper Peninsula residents and the tourists who come to the taprooms and brewpubs have gotten pretty knowledgeable and sophisticated." Two more craft breweries will be open when I return to the cabin next spring. I will look forward to visiting them and, of course, to renewing acquaintances whose ales and lagers I'd so enjoyed sipping on the dock of the bay.

The fire had died down to embers. Tomorrow, when I'd be leaving my little cabin in the big woods to return to Albuquerque, I'd be taking a few six-packs of my favorite UP beers with me, along with wonderful memories of my travels along the Ale Trails of Michigan's Upper Peninsula.

Appendix 1 - Directory of
Upper Peninsula Breweries

The directory includes all breweries open as of January 1, 2023. "Core beer list" includes beers available year-round, seasonal releases, and others that are frequently available. (Note that brewers frequently drop beers from their lists and add new ones. For a brewery's up-to-date list of beers, check its FaceBook page or check www.untappd.com.)

The word "menu" following "food" signifies that the taproom or brewpub has a food menu and that patrons are not permitted to bring food into the establishment. "BYOF" means "bring your own food." Patrons are welcome to bring food into or order food to be delivered to the brewery taproom. Food trucks are often parked outside many of the breweries. Growlers are 64 or 32 ounce glass jars that are filled and capped at a brewery's taproom. Crowlers are 32 ounce aluminum cans that are filled and sealed at a brewery's taproom.

The information about individual breweries will be updated each May and published in the author's beer blog: www.beerquestwest.com.

CRAFT BREWERIES AND BREWPUBS BY LOCATION

Alpha
- Alpha Michigan Brewing Company

Calumet
- Red Jacket Brewing Company at Michigan House Café

Cedarville
- Les Cheneaux Distillers

Cooks
- LaTulip Brewing Company

Copper Harbor
- Brickside Brewery

Escanaba
- Hereford & Hops Steakhouse and Brewpub
- Upper Hand Brewery

Grand Marais
- Lake Superior Brewing Company at Dunes Saloon

Harvey
- Lake Superior Smokehouse Brewpub

Houghton
- Copper Country Brewing Company at the Library Restaurant
- Keweenaw Brewing Company (brewery and taproom)

Ironwood
- Cold Iron Brewing

Ishpeming
- Cognition Brewing Company
- Jasper Ridge Brewery and Restaurant

Kingsford
- 51st State Brewing Company

Manistique
- Flatiron Brewing Company (scheduled to open spring 2023)

Marenisco
- Five Sons Brewing Company

Marquette
- Barrel + Beam Brewing Company
- Blackrocks Brewery

- Drifa Brewing Company
- Kognisjon Bryggeri (scheduled to open spring 2023)
- Marquette Harbor Brewery at Vierling Restaurant
- Ore Dock Brewing Company
- Superior Culture

Menominee
- Three Bridge Brewing Company

Munising
- ByGeorge Brewing Company
- East Channel Brewing Company

Negaunee
- Upper Peninsula Brewing Company

Sault Ste Marie
- Soo Brewing Company

South Range
- Keweenaw Brewing Company (production brewery)

Tahquamenon Falls (Upper Falls)
- Tahquamenon Falls Brewery and Pub at Camp 33

㉔ 51ˢᵀ STATE BREWING COMPANY

115 Harding Ave, Kingsford, MI 49802
906-828-2167
www.51ststatebrewingco.com
www.facebook.com/51stStateBrewingCo
Opened: 2018
Principal owners: Jeff Brickey, Victoria Brickey
Brewer: Jeff Brickey
Brewery size: 4 barrels
Flagship beer: Batty Millie Blueberry Wheat Ale
Core beer list: State of Superior American Pale Ale, 3 Vagabonds Light American Lager, Batty Millie Blueberry Wheat, GC-RA Porter, On Island Time New England IPA, Woody Wagon Scotch Ale, Ski Jump American IPA, Tropical Milkshake New England IPA, Never Was Cream Ale, My Redheaded Cousin Amber/Red, Winter Torpor Belgian Strong Ale, St. Patrick's Purgatory Irish Dry Stout, Coconut Mango IPA, Peanut Butter Cup Stout, Fusti Lugs Chocolate/ Coconut Porter
Available in draft, growlers, crowlers
Distribution area: western Upper Peninsula, northeastern Wisconsin
On-site: food -- menu; off-sales; souvenirs; family friendly; ADA compliant

㉓ ALPHA MICHIGAN BREWING COMPANY

303 East Center St, Alpha, MI 49902
920-358-9551
www.alphamibeer.com, www.facebook.com/alphamibeer
Opened: 2018
Principal owners: Mary Bjork, Mike Bjork, Julie Creel, Stu Creel
Brew crew: Mike Bjork, Stu Creel, Lydia Novitsky, Lars Anderson
Brewery size: 3barrels
Flagship Beers: Naughty School Girl Cream Ale, Brule River Red
Core beer list: Brule River Red, Banana Split Porter, Bear's Cave American IPA, Naughty School Girl Cream Ale, Pandemic Pilsner, Spring Ahead Double IPA, Biere de Jean Nicolet (Belgium Oat Lager), What's It About Irish Stout, Book Mine Brown Ale, Blood Orange Spring Saison, Krystal Kolsch, Mastodon Mash Red Double IPA, Kallawalla Wit, Porter School Porter, Blueberry Muffin Wheat Beer

Available in draft, growlers, crowlers, cans, bag of beer (biodegradable bags)

Distribution area: east central Upper Peninsula

On-site: food – snacks, Thursday pasties, Friday fish fry, Saturday pizza, BYOF; off-sales; souvenirs; family friendly; pet friendly on patio; ADA compliant

⓭ BARREL + BEAM BREWING COMPANY

260 Northwoods Rd, Marquette, MI 49855
906-273-2559
www.barrelandbeam.com, www.facebook.com/barrelandbeam

Opened: 2018

Principal owners: Nick Van Court, Marina Dupler

Brew crew: Nick Van Court, Joe Thierry, Eamon Ketchum

Brewery size: 10 barrels

Flagship beer: Terre à Terre Saison

Core beer list: Terre à Terre Saison, Star-Eyed Sour-Fruited Ale (pears), Blanc Du Nord Wit, Heritage Saison, Petit Saison, Terroir Saison, , Spooky Kriek Cherry Lambic, Golden Partager Saison, Tart Barrel Aged Saison (Biere de Coupage), Acer Stout, Star Plum Stout, Arcadian Connection Wild Beer, Pret Grisette, Bliss Barrel Aged Saison

Available in draft, bottles, cans, growlers

Distribution area: Wisconsin, Michigan

On-site: food -- menu; off-sales; souvenirs; family friendly; pets in beer garden; ADA compliant

⓫ BLACKROCKS BREWERY

424 North Third St, Marquette, MI 49855 (pub)
950 West Washington St, Marquette, MI 49855 (production brewery – not open to public)
906-273-1333 (pub), 906-273-1240 (brewery)
www.blackrocksbrewery.com,
www.facebook.com/BlackrocksBrewery

Opened: 2010

Principal owners: Andy Langlois, David Manson

Brew crew: Andrew Reeves, Christopher Hutte, Charles Hotelling, Evan Garret, Alex Leckie, Ethan Van Lente, Neil Washburn, Stephan Wolf

Brewery size: 20 barrels (production brewery), 1 barrel and 3 barrels (pub)
Flagship beer: 51K IPA
Core beer list: 51K American IPA, MyKiss IPA American IPA, Grand Rabbits Cream Ale, Coconut Brown Ale, Honey Lav Wheat Ale, Hiawatha American Wheat Ale, Presque Ale American Pale Ale, Starman American Pale Ale, Nordskye Session IPA, Noops New England IPA, Super Deluxe German Helles, Oktoberfest Marzen, Float Copper Amber Lager, Classic Pilsner, Barrel Aged Barbaric Yawp Scotch Ale
Available in draft, growlers, crowlers, cans
Distribution area: Michigan, Wisconsin
On-site (pub only): food -- snacks, food trucks, BYOF; off-sales, souvenirs; family friendly, ADA compliant

⑰ BRICKSIDE BREWERY

64 Gratiot Street, Copper Harbor, MI 49918
906-289-4772
www.bricksidebrewery.com
Opened: 2012
Owners: Jason Robinson, Jessica Robinson
Brewer: Jason Robinson
Brewery size: 3 barrels
Flagship beer: Double Up Hill IPA
Core beer list: Jackpine Savage ESB, Quincy Brown, Fine Day Pale Ale, Uphill Both Ways Double IPA, UP IPA, Park Bench Porter, Walter's Weizen, Superior Wit, Red Metal Amber, Farm Beer Saison, Some IPA
Available in draft, growlers
Distribution area: on-site only
On-site: food: brewery-owned food truck on-site: off-sales; souvenirs; family friendly; pet friendly- patio; ADA accessible

❻ BYGEORGE BREWING COMPANY

231 East Superior St, Munising, MI 49862
906-387-2739
bygeorgebrewing.com, www.facebook.com/bygeorgebrewing
Opened: 2020
Principal owners: George Schultz, Matt Johnson

Brew crew: George Schultz, Matt Johnson, Gabe Niven
Brewery size: 7 barrels
Flagship Beers: Walking with Giants Apricot Blonde Ale, Maize N Grace Light Lager, Elephant Disco IPA, Nighthawk Oryx Beer
Core beer list: Maize N Grace American Light Lager, Elephant Disco American IPA, Walking with Giants Apricot Blonde Ale, Nighthawk Onyx Beer, Schultz Bier (Marzen), Alger Cloudy Hefeweizen, Snow Pants Romance Wit, Hiawatha Broth American Pale Ale,Writer's Bock, Moody Ruby's Red Cluster Fugget Red Lager, Unicorn Piss New England IPA, Yooperdorf Alt Beer, Leader of the Patch Strawberry Milkshake IPA
Available in draft, growlers, cans
Distribution area: Alger County, Marquette County
On-site: food -- menu, off-sales, souvenirs; family friendly, pet friendly (patio only), ADA compliant

⓯ COGNITION BREWING COMPANY

113 East Canda Street, Ishpeming, MI 49849
906-204-2724
www.cognitionbrewingcompany.com,
www.facebook.com/CognitionBrewingCompany
Brewery opened: 2015
Principal owner: Jay Clancey
Brew crew: Kris Thompson, Justin Boldenow
Brewery size: 7 barrels and 1 barrel pilot system
Flagship beer: Gnome Wrecker Belgian Style Pale Ale
Core beer list: The Grace of Faded Things Gose, Octopus Was Very Scary Imperial Stout, Psybient American IPA, Desolate Cosmos Schwarzbier, Zombie King Red Ale, Flower and Dean Cream Ale, Storm to Castle Scotch Ale, Gnome Wrecker Belgian Style Pale Ale, Oblivion Milk Stout, Deep Scream Cream Ale, Bloody Scream Pale Ale, Fjordlands Pilsner, Graven-Tosk Gravol Smoked Stout, Midnattsol Sahti, Pombluegenesis Kettle Sour Berliner Weisse Style Blueberry Ale
Available in draft, growlers, crowlers
Distribution area: Michigan
On-site: food -- snacks, BYOF; off-sales; souvenirs; family friendly; pet friendly-outside, ADA compliant

㉑ COLD IRON BREWING

104 South Lowell St, Ironwood, MI 49938
906-285-7020
www.coldironbrewing.com, www.facebook.com/coldironbrewing
Opened: 2017
Principal owners: John Garske, Andy Warren, Bob Burchell, Tom Bergman, Will Andersen, Cody Mukavitz, Scott Erikson, Chris Patritto
Brewer: Andy Warren
Brewery size: 3 barrels
Flagship beer: Drift North American IPA
Core beer list: Ice Out Maple Scotch Ale, Ayer Street Amber, Mosaic Blonde Ale, Michiconsin Honey Cream Ale, Porcupine Light Lager, Sleight American Stout, Drift North American IPA, Black River Dark Ale, Warming Hut Wee Heavy Scotch Ale, Drift South Jalapeno American Pale Ale, Heat Wave Hefeweizen, Blue Collar Kolsch, Oktoberfest, Jack Frost Doppelboch, Axel's Alt Bier, Catherine the Great Porter
Available in draft, growlers, crowlers, cans
Distribution area: on-site only
On-site: food – snacks, BYOF; off-sales; souvenirs; family friendly; pet friendly; ADA compliant

⑲ COPPER COUNTRY BREWING COMPANY
at THE LIBRARY RESTAURANT

62 Isle Royale St, Houghton, MI 49931
906-481-2665
www.thelibraryhoughton.com
www.facebook.com/thelibraryhoughton
Brewery opened originally in 1997—reopened in 2019 as Copper Country Brewing Company
Principal owner: Tom Romps
Brewer: Bob Jackson, Christian Maki
Brewery size: 5 barrels
Flagship beer: Copper Country Gold
Core beer list: Rice Lake Blueberry Ale, Devil's Washtub Double IPA, Husky American Pale Ale, Rock Harbor Blonde Light Ale, Copper Country Gold American Wheat, Red Ridge Rye Ale, Miners

American IPA, Bete Grise Brown Ale, Sturgeon River Dry Stout, White City Hefeweizen
Available in draft, growlers, crowlers
Distribution area: on-site only
On-site: food -- menu; off-sales; souvenirs; family friendly; ADA compliant

⑧ DRIFA BREWING COMPANY

501 South Lake St, Marquette, MI 49855
906-273-1300
www.drifabrewing.beer, www.facebook.com/drifabrewing
Opened: 2019
Principal owners: Marquette Brewing Cooperative
Brew crew: Spencer Trubac, Alex Perkins
Brewery size: twin 2 barrels
Core beer list: Walk of Shame Coffee Brown Ale, Spindrift Ginger Wheat Ale, Never-ending Squawk Amber Ale, Lower Harbor American Lager, Green Ladder American IPA, In Irons Hefeweizen, Farmer Queen American Stout, Pigeon Feathers Cream Ale, Judy's Big Booty Hazy IPA, Booksellers Folly Imperial IPA, Sustadt Alt
Available in draft, kegs, growlers, crowlers, cans
Distribution area: on-site only
On-site: food -- snacks, BYOF; off-sales; souvenirs; family friendly; pet friendly -- patio only; ADA complaint

⑤ EAST CHANNEL BREWING COMPANY

209 Maple St, Munising, MI, 49862
906-387-3007
www.eastchannelbrewery.com,
www.facebook.com/EastChannelBrew
Opened: 2016
Principal owners: Joe DesJardins, Ted Majewski
Brew crew: Joe DesJardins, Ted Majewski
Brewery size: 3.5 barrels
Flagship beer: Old Tru's IPA
Core beer list: Old Tru's American IPA, Lake Street Oatmeal Stout, Speedball Tucker New England IPA, Hobo Nectar American Light Lager, Island's Grand as Always Blood Orange Hefeweizen, Paradise Waitin' Blueberry Lager, Portside Red Ale, Widdlestick S'More Coffee Stout, Happy Thoughts American Pale Ale, Uncle

Peanut's Peanut and Cocoa Porter, Sapster Maple Double IPA, East Channel Harry Bert's Brown Ale, Fake News Tart Cherry IPA
Available in draft, growlers, cans
Distribution area: Upper Peninsula
On-site: food – pizza (summer only), BYOF; off sales; souvenirs; family friendly; ADA compliant

㉒ FIVE SONS BREWING COMPANY

236 Main St, Marenisco, MI, 49947
906-787-2000
www.fivesonsbrewingmi.com
www.facebook.com/fivesonsbrewingmarenisco
Opened: 2022
Owner: Bruce Mahler
Brewer: Bruce Mahler
Brewery size: 3 barrels
Flagship Beers: Honey Ope's Cream Ale, Bee Sting Honey Jalapeno Wheat Beer, Kraftig Oatmeal Vanilla Stout
Core beer list: Honey Ope's Cream Ale, Cheerio English Bitter ESB, Quails Irish Red, Milltown Noble Kolsch, Alligator Eye-PA English IPA, Kraftig Oatmeal Vanilla Stout, Bee Sting Honey Jalapeno Wheat Beer
Available in draft, growlers, crowlers
Distribution: on-site only
On-site: food -- snacks, BYOF; off-sales; souvenirs; family friendly; pet friendly – patio only; ADA compliant

㉙ FLATIRON BREWING COMPANY

375 Traders Point Dr Stop # 4, Manistique, MI 49854
616-500-3838
www.flatiron-brewing.com, www.facebook.com/FlatironBrewing
Opening Spring 2023
Principal owners: Jake Boudreau, Nick Powers, Adam Popour, Mark Osgerby, Ben Pineau
Brewer: Ben Miller
Brewery Size: 4 barrel
Core beer list: intend to open with an American Lager, American IPA, Hazy IPA, Kettle Corn Stout, Strawberry Rhubarb Belgian
Available in draft and growlers
Distribution area: on-site

On-site: food – menu; off-sales; souvenirs; family friendly, ADA compliant

㉗ HEREFORD & HOPS STEAKHOUSE AND BREWPUB

624 Ludington St, Escanaba, MI 49829
906-789-1945
www.herefordandhops.com, www.facebook.com/HerefordandHops
Opened: 1994
Principal Owner: Rebecca Moody
Brewer: Mike Sattem
Brewery size: 7 barrels
Flagship beer: Redemption IPA
Core beer list: Bluegrass Blueberry Wheat Ale, Whitetail Golden Ale, Soleil American Wheat Ale, Redemption American IPA, Highlander Wee Heavy Scotch Ale, Cleary Irish Red Ale, Blackbird Oatmeal Stout, Les Sentiels Kolsch Ale, Fest Bier Marzen, Whitewalker IPA, Maibock, Nut Brown Ale, Hefeweizen, Schwarzbier, Stumpsitter Stout, Choco-Razz Stout, Alt Bier
Available in draft, growlers
Distribution area: on-site only
On-site: food -- menu; off-sales; souvenirs; family friendly; pet friendly -- on patio; ADA compliant

⑯ JASPER RIDGE BREWERY AND RESTAURANT

1075 Country Lane, Ishpeming, MI 49849
906-485-6017
jasperridgebrewery.com, www.facebook.com/JasperRidgeBrewery
Opened: 1996
Principal owners: Brad Argall, Michelle LaMere
Brew crew: Kevin Hokenson, John Silverstone, Tina Alred
Flagship beer: Rope's Golden Wheat
Core beer list: Blastin' Blueberry Wheat Ale, Rope's Golden Wheat Ale, Wayward Blonde Ale, Bonfire Smoked Porter, Marzen/Oktoberfest, Soultaker Red Ale, IPA (New England IPA), Cherry Blonde Ale, Double Frozen Auger Imperial IPA, Driftwood Pale Ale, WunderDust American IPA, Copper Kolsch, Jasper Brown Ale, Slugworth Chocolate Stout, Attack Penguin IPA
Available in draft, growlers, cans
Distribution area: on-site only

On-site: food -- menu; off-sales; souvenirs; family friendly; ADA compliant

⑳ KEWEENAW BREWING COMPANY

Production brewery: 10 Fourth St, South Range, MI 49963
906-482-1937
www.kbc.beer, www.facebook.com/keweenawbrewing
Taproom: 408 Shelden Avenue, Houghton, MI 49931, 906-482-5596
Opened: 2004
Principal owners: Dick Gray, Paul Boissevain
Brew crew: Tom Duex, Luke Dedo
Brewery size: 60 barrels (production brewery), 12 barrels (tap room)
Flagship beers: Widow Maker Black Ale, Pick Axe Blonde Ale Core beer list: Widow Maker Black Ale, Pick Axe Blonde Ale, Red Jacket Amber Ale, Point Trail Rye Pale Ale, Borealis Broo Coffee Amber Ale, November Gale American Pale, Hefe Royale Hefeweizen, Level 92 Black IPA, Olde Ore Dock Scottish Ale, UP Witbier, Lift Bridge Brown Ale, Early Autumn Oktoberfest, Red Ridge Blood Orange Ale, Keweenaw Belle Blueberry Wheat Ale
Available in draft, cans, growlers, crowlers
Distribution area: Michigan, northern Wisconsin, northern Minnesota
On-site (tap room): food -- snacks, BYOF; off-sales; souvenirs; family friendly; pet friendly – outside deck only; ADA compliant

❹ LAKE SUPERIOR BREWING COMPANY at DUNES SALOON

N 14283 Lake Ave, Grand Marais, MI 49839
906-494-2337
www.grandmaraismichigan.com/business-directory/
www.facebook.com/LakeSuperiorBrewing
Opened: 1994
Owner: Chris Sarver
Brewer: Sean DeWitt
Brewery size: 5.5 barrels
Flagship beers: Blueberry Wheat Ale, Sandstone American Pale Ale
Core beer list: Sandstone American Pale Ale, Cabin Fever ESB, Blueberry Wheat Ale, Hematite Stout, Granite Brown Ale, Puddingstone Wheat Ale, Backwoods Blonde Ale, Steelhead Red

IPA, October Rust Altbier, First Creek Kolsch, Hazelnut Brown Ale, Hindsight American IPA, Hefeweizen, Southpaw Session IPA
Available in draft, growlers
Distribution: on-site only
On-site: food -- menu; off-sales; souvenirs; family friendly; pet friendly – patio only

❼ LAKE SUPERIOR SMOKEHOUSE BREWPUB

200 West Main St, Harvey, MI 49855
906-273-0952
www.lakesuperiorsmokehouse.com,
www.facebook.com/lakesuperiorsmokehousepub
Opened: 2019
Principal owner: Scott Arbour
Brew crew: Kyle Peterson, Scott Arbour
Brewery size: 5 barrels
Flagship beer: Blueberry Wheat Ale
Core Beer List: Lake Superior Blueberry Wheat Ale, Old Foggy Red Ale, LLSP Midnight Black Ale, LLSP Blueberry Wheat Ale, Golden Blonde Ale, Lake Superior Harvey Haze New England IPA, Hoppy Days American IPA, Belgian Wit, So Long Saison
Available in draft, crowlers, growlers
Distribution: on-site only
On-site: food -- menu; off-sales; souvenirs; family friendly; pet friendly – outside beer garden; ADA compliant

㉘ LATULIP BREWING COMPANY

11858W US Highway 2, Cooks, MI 49817
906-644-2317
www.facebook.com/latulipbrewingco
Opened: 2022
Owners: Jeff LaTulip, Jason LaTulip
Brewers: Jeff LaTulip, Jason LaTulip
Core beer List: Blonde Ale, Irish Red Ale, Light Lager, Stout, Cucumber Sour, Farmhouse Ale, American IPA.
Available in draft, growlers, crowlers, cans
Distribution area: Delta, Schoolcraft Counties
On-site: food: snacks -- BYOF; off-sales; souvenirs; family friendly; pet friendly -- in beer garden; ADA compliant

❶ LES CHENEAUX DISTILLERS

172 South Meridian St, Cedarville, MI 49719
906-484-1213
www.lescheneauxdistillers.com,
www.facebook.com/lescheneauxdistillers
Opened: 2017
Principal owners: Jason Bohn, Kirsten Bohn; Jay Bowlby, Sue Bowlby
Brew crew: Jay Bowlby, Peter Duman, Kevin Hill
Brewery size: 5 barrels
Flagship beer: Buoy Tipper Blonde Imperial Pilsner
Core Beer List: Buoy Tipper Blonde Imperial Pilsner, Buoy Beacon Pilsner, Moon Over Mackinac Witbier, Vera B's Honey Brown Ale, Redheaded Stepchild Red Ale, Northern Tropics Session IPA, Navigator American Pale Ale, Island Hopper Double IPA, Black Sails Black IPA, Dark Side of the Brew Stout, Arborvitae Amber Ale, Dolomite Dunkelweisen, Maple Bourbon Barrel Aged Stout, Vanilla Porter, Dingo Blueberry Wheat Beer
Available in draft, kegs, growlers, crowlers
Distribution area: Eastern Upper Peninsula, Northern Lower Peninsula
On-site: food -- menu; off-sales; souvenirs; family friendly; ADA compliant

❾ MARQUETTE HARBOR BREWERY
at THE VIERLING RESTAURANT

119 South Front St, Marquette, MI 49855
906-228-3533
www.facebook.com/TheVierling
Opened: 1995 (brewery); 1985 (restaurant)
Principal owners: Terry Doyle, Kristi Doyle
Brewer: Derek "Chumley" Anderson
Brewery size: 5 barrels
Flagship beer: Blueberry Wheat Ale
Core beer list: Blonde Ale, Tart Cherry Wheat Ale, Blueberry Wheat Ale, Peach Wheat Ale, American Pale Ale, Honey Porter, Yooper Red Ale, Stout, Honey Wheat Ale, Laid Back American IPA, Chum's Double Pale Ale
Available in draft, growlers
Distribution: on-site only

On-site: food -- menu; off-sales; souvenirs; family friendly; ADA compliant

⑩ ORE DOCK BREWING COMPANY

114 Spring St, Marquette, MI 49855
906-228-8888
www.oredockbrewing.com, www.facebook.com/OreDock
Opened: 2012
Principal owners: Andrea Pernsteiner, Wes Pernsteiner
Brew crew: Jake Shea, Greg Hobson, Douglas Bellinger, Chuck Keely
Brewery size: 10 barrels
Flagship beer: Reclamation IPA
Core beer list: Reclamation American IPA, Berserker Hazy New England IPA, Queen City Kolsch , Uncle Drew's Flying Machine New England Pale Ale, Porter (American Robust), Bum's Beach American Wheat Ale, Saison, Blond, Bramble on Rose Belgian Golden Strong Ale, Six Pointer Munich Dunkel, Blue Canoe Blueberry Berliner Weisse
Available in draft, cans, growlers
Distribution area: Michigan
On-site: Food -- BYOF; off-sales; souvenirs; family friendly; pet friendly – patio only; ADA compliant

⑱ RED JACKET BREWING COMPANY at MICHIGAN HOUSE CAFÉ

300 Sixth St, Calumet, MI 49913
906-337-1910
www.michiganhousecafe.com,
Brewery opened: 2005
Principal Owners: Tim Bies, Sue Bies
Brewer: Brian Hess
Brewery size: 3 barrels.
Flagship beer: Oatmeal Espress Stout
Core beer list: Keweenaw Cowboy American IPA, Our Brown Ale, Oatmeal Espress Stout, Smooth Trail American Pale Ale, Wee Heavy Scotch Ale, Syla Belgian Tripel
Available in draft, growlers
Distribution area: on-site only
On-site: food -- menu; off-sales; souvenirs; family friendly; ADA compliant

➋ SOO BREWING COMPANY and 1668 WINERY

100 West Portage Ave, Sault Ste Marie, MI 49783
906-259-5035
www. soobrew.com, www.facebook.com/SooBrew
Opened: 2011
Principal Owners: Ray Bauer, Joan Bauer
Brewer: Ray Bauer
Brewery size: 3.5 barrels.
Flagship beer: Maggie's Irish Red
Core beer List: a rotating beer list, with many beers appearing regularly during the year. Maggie's Irish Red Ale, 13 American IPA, Laker Gold Blonde Ale, Huskador New England IPA, Tiramisu Stout, Braveheart Stout, Soo Wheeat! Raspberry Wheat Ale, Soo Grand Cru Belgian Wit, Soo Brew English Mild Ale, Cup of the Day Porter, 810 Brown Ale, The Legend Dortmunder Lager, Crystal Blue Persuasion Blueberry Wheat Ale
Available in draft, growlers, cans
Distribution area: eastern UP
On-site: food -- menu; off-sales; souvenirs; family friendly; pet friendly – on patio; ADA compliant

⓬ SUPERIOR CULTURE

717 North Third St., Marquette, MI 49855
906-273-0927
www.superiorculturemqt.com,
www.facebook.com/superiorculturemqt
Opened: 2018 (brewery)
Principal owner: Alex Rowland
Brew crew: Alex Rowland, Caden Reed, Cole Stefl
Brewery size: 55 gallon fermenters
Flagship beer: Ginger Beer
Core beer list: Raspberry Chocolate Ale, Choco Cherry Brown, Wildberry Ginger Beer, Birch Beer Blonde Ale, UP Maple Porter, Honey Booch American Pale Ale
Available in draft, growlers, bottles
Distribution area: Upper Peninsula
On-site: food -- snacks, BYOF; off-sales; souvenirs; family friendly; pet friendly; ADA compliant

❸ TAHQUAMENON FALLS BREWERY AND PUB AT CAMP 33

24019 Upper Falls Drive, Paradise, MI 49768 (site address)
906-492-3300
www.tahquamenonfallsbrewery.com
Opened: 1996
Principal Owner: Lark Ludlow
Brewster: Lark Ludlow
Brewery Size: 10 barrels
Core beer list: (a rotating beer list with four beers available at any given time). Lumberjack Pale American Lager, Falls Tannin American Red Ale , Harvest Wheat American Wheat Ale, Birdseye Maple Ale, Summer Wheat Ale, Black Bear Stout, Porcupine English Pale Ale, Raspberry Wheat Ale (Wit), White Pine Pilsner, Blueberry Wheat Ale, Honey Brown Ale, Wolverine Wheat Ale
Available in: draft
Distribution area: on-site only
On-site: food -- menu; gift shop; family friendly; pet friendly-- on patio; ADA compliant

㉕ THREE BRIDGE BREWING COMPANY

2221 Thirteenth St, Menominee, MI 49858
906-399-9611
www.facebook.com/threebridgebrewing
Opened: 2018
Owners: Kristoffer Rusch, Sarah Rusch
Brewer crew: Kristoffer Rusch, Sarah Rusch
Brewery size: 7 barrels
Flagship beers: Sky Kettle Marzen, Stuttgart German Helles
Core beer list: Sky Kettle Marzen, Beno Fino Coffee Stout, River Coast Imperial IPA, Cranky Dwarf Sour Ale, Dreamwalker American IPA, Tree Shaker Stout, Never Settle for Weiss Hefeweizen, Flower Hunter American IPA, Angler's Brown Ale, Flirty Mousse Cream Ale, Stuttgart German Helles, Excursion Zone American IPA, Basic Bitches Blueberry Ale, Belly Warmer Winter Lager, Death Candle Pumpkin Pie Ale, Inner Earth Double IPA, Lovely Lady Pina Colada Ale
Available in: draft, growlers
Distribution area: on-site only
On-site: food -- BYOF; off-sales; souvenirs; family friendly; pet friendly; ADA compliant

㉖ UPPER HAND BREWERY

3525 Airport Rd, Escanaba, MI 49829
906-233-5005
www.upperhandbrewery.com,
www.facebook.co/UpperHandBrewery
Opened: 2014
Principal owner: New Belgium Brewing Company
Brew crew: Jesse Herman, Tim Otis, Jose Luis Cortés Rosado, Tim Schaaf, Brett Taylor, Tim DeClaire, Dakota Soule, Kirk Kaurala
Brewery size: 20 barrels
Flagship beer: UPA (Upper Peninsula Ale)
Core beer list: Lager, Yooper American Pale Ale, IPA, Upper Peninsula Pale Ale, Deer Camp Amber Lager, Laughing Fish Golden Ale, Wapatooie! Fruit Beer, Sisu Stout, Lumen India Pale Lager, Red Buck Red IPA, Nowhere Land Wheat Beer
Available in draft, cans, crowlers
Distribution area: Michigan
On-site: food – snacks, BYOF; off-sales; souvenirs; family friendly; pet friendly -- on patio; ADA compliant

⑭ UPPER PENINSULA BREWING COMPANY

342 Rail Street, Negaunee, MI 49866
906-475-8722
www.upperpeninsulabrewingcompany.com,
www.facebook.com/UPbrewingcompany
Opened: 2022
Principal owners: Jim Kantola, Ann Kantola
Brewer: Mason Mathis
Brewery size: 3.5 barrels
Flagship beer: Solsken American Wheat
Core beer list: Trail 8 Blonde Ale (Belgian), Solsken American Wheat, JRA Belgian Pale, Sunny Dew Hazy New England IPA, Saison, Rose Eh! Oenobeer Belgian Ale (hibiscus, grapes), Coppertown Amber Ale, Loop-Garou Belgian Stout (with chocolate), Golden Gurl Belgian Strong Ale, Hey Buddy #2 Belgian Wheat Ale with Cranberries
Available in: draft, kegs, growlers, kegs
Distribution area: western UP
On-site: food -- snacks, BYOF; off-sales; souvenirs; family friendly; pet friendly -- on patio; ADA compliant

Appendix 2 - From Grain to Glass: Brewing, Packaging, and Drinking Beer

The Big Four: Basic Ingredients

Water, malted grain, hops, and yeast.

For centuries, these ingredients have been used to brew beer. Because there are different types of each ingredient and the four can be combined in a variety of ways, they can be used to create dozens of different styles of beer. (See Appendix 3: A Guide to Beer Styles.)

Throughout the twentieth century, beer advertising frequently emphasized water to stress the purity and the crisp, clean flavor of the beer. For example, Olympia Brewing proclaimed "It's the water" and made much of the artesian wells that lay beneath the facility in Tumwater, Washington. Ore Dock of Marquette advertises that their beers are "What water wants to be." Of course, water is important—it makes up at least 90 percent of a glass or bottle of beer. Brewers call it "liquor," and five litres of it are required for each litre of beer produced. In addition to the water content of the product, water is used in the brewing process and in the vigorous cleaning of equipment.

The relative hardness or softness of water influences the taste of the beverage, and, before the twentieth century, certain styles emerged because of the composition of the water close to a brewery. The hard water of England's Burton-on-Trent contributed to the distinctive taste of the pale ales brewed there; the soft water in Pilsen, Czech Republic (then called Bohemia), was an important element of its acclaimed lagers. Now, scientific techniques enable brewers to alter tap water so that it possesses the qualities needed for whatever style they may be brewing. The process is called "building water."

Malt supplies the fermentable sugars that become the alcohol in beer. It is made when kernels of grain (usually barley, but sometimes wheat or rye) are steeped in water until they germinate;

they are then dried and roasted in kilns. During the process, insoluble starches are converted into the soluble starches and sugars essential to the brewing process. By using different strains of grain and kilning at different and varying temperatures, many kinds of malt are produced, each one helping to create a style of beer with a distinctive color, flavor, and aroma. For example, Vienna malt, which is gold in color, adds nutty, toasty notes to beer. Chocolate malts can create a flavor that seems slightly burnt. And amber malts evoke the flavors of toffee and bread. Some very large brewing companies replace a portion of the malts with such less expensive adjuncts as corn and rice, which also contain fermentable sugars.

Hops, the cone-shaped "flowers" of a plant related to cannabis, have lupulin glands that contain alpha acids. These alpha acids produce a bitterness that balances the sweeter malt tastes in beer, often create citrusy or floral aromas and flavors, and act as preservatives. In fact, when the British shipped beer to colonial officials in India, they used heavy doses of hops to help it survive the long sea journey. With over 100 varieties of hops available, it is not surprising that the various hop extracts, powders, pellets, and whole flowers used in brewers' recipes (usually at a ratio of one part to over thirty parts of malt) have been called the spices of brewing. What are often referred to as the "C hops"—Cascade, Centennial, and Chinook—have been regularly used by craft brewers in their very popular India pale ales. The "noble hops"—Hallertau, Saaz, and Tettnang, to name three—are used by brewers to create the crisp and delicate bitterness that characterize German- and Bohemian-style pilsners. Most beer recipes call for the use of hop pellets. However, in recent years, freshly harvested hops are very quickly transported to a nearby brewery and used to create beers that are often called "fresh-hopped" or "wet-hopped."

Some modern brewers complement or replace a portion of the hops in a recipe with herbs that, before the widespread use of hops in the latter Middle Ages, were used to contribute bitterness and flavor to beer. Some of the bittering and aroma ingredients being used include spruce tips, nettles, and clary sage.

Yeasts, one-celled micro-organisms, are essential to the brewing of beer. Without them there would be no beer, just a flat, malt-flavored, non-alcoholic beverage. Yeasts feed on the fermentable sugars derived from malt or adjuncts and produce alcohol and carbon dioxide as "waste materials." Medieval monks, who brewed what was to them liquid sustenance, referred to yeast as "Godisgood." Early brewers often depended on airborne, invisible strains of this divine gift to alight on their liquid and work its heavenly miracles. Some modern breweries place wort in a large open vessel called a coolship where it is exposed to airborne yeasts.

Yeast was first specifically identified in the seventeenth century, and, in the nineteenth century, the research of French scientist Louis Pasteur made possible the isolation and development of over one hundred strains that are used in brewing. In addition to producing alcohol, each strain of yeast contributes a different flavor to the beer. This is particularly the case in Belgian-style beers, where the yeast contributes to the characteristic sour and funky tastes.

As well as these four basics, brewers sometimes include such ingredients as spices, fruits or fruit extracts, honey, maple syrup, and even spruce needles or juniper berries. Called additives, as distinct from adjuncts, these items do not generally influence the alcohol content of beer, but contribute additional flavors to the basic ones created by the interactions of the water, malts, hops, and yeast. When beers are aged in wooden barrels, they often acquire subtle traces of the rums, whiskies, wines, or other alcoholic beverages that had previously been stored in the vessels. The type of wood out of which the barrels are made (usually oak) also influences flavor.

Brewing and Brewing Equipment

Brewing begins after the brewer chooses a specific recipe, gathers the appropriate ingredients, and, perhaps most important, makes sure that the brewing equipment is clean—very, very clean. Without completely sanitized equipment, the possibilities of creating bad, spoiled beer are increased greatly.

The first step is **milling** chunks of malt into grist, which is then deposited in a large metal vessel called a **mash tun**, where it is mixed with water that is heated to around 150 degrees Fahrenheit. In the resulting "porridge" or **mash**, the malt's starches are converted into fermentable sugars. The mash is strained, and the **wort**, the sugar water, placed in a **brew kettle**, to be vigorously boiled for between one and two hours. This process sterilizes the liquid and helps prevent contamination. During the boil, hops are added. The boil completed, the hop residue is separated and the liquid passed through a **heat exchange unit** where it is quickly cooled.

At this point, the liquid is essentially malt-and-hop-flavored water. However, after it is transferred to a **fermentation tank** and yeast is added, the wort's transformation into beer begins. Within eight to ten hours, the process of fermentation is well under way. For ales, which are made with top-fermenting yeast, the temperature in the fermentation tank is kept between sixty and seventy degrees Fahrenheit; for lagers, which use bottom-fermenting yeast, the tanks are kept around forty-eight degrees Fahrenheit. The fermentation period for ales is a week to ten days; for lagers, between three and four weeks. After fermentation is complete, the now alcoholic beverage is transferred to **conditioning or aging tanks** to mature. Ales are conditioned for up to two weeks, lagers for six weeks or more. At this point, the beer is ready to be delivered from the tanks to taps in a brewpub, or to be packaged in kegs, bottles, or cans.

Packaging Beer

For centuries, people took a pitcher or small bucket to the local pub or tavern, where they had it filled with beer to take home. Late in the nineteenth century, when glass became cheaper to manufacture, beer began to be bottled, and after World War II, tin and later aluminum cans became the preferred containers for beer. Before the widespread availability of bottles, most beer was consumed away from the home. After that, consumption shifted to the home. Beer ads in the 1950s showed well-dressed adults enjoying a cool one in their living rooms. When breweries became major sponsors of weekend televised sports, much beer was consumed by armchair athletes sitting in front of the television. And then, as satellite and paid television became available later in the twentieth century, sports bars began to spring up, all of them with numerous television sets, each tuned to a different game. The consumption of beer outside the home was making a comeback. In recent years, taprooms have become like the old British pubs, "locals" where locals and tourists alike gathered to enjoy good beer, good conversation, and often good music by local musicians.

When the craft brewing revolution began in the late 1970s, purists insisted that bottles were the only acceptable containers. Cans, they said, gave beer a funny taste, and, perhaps more important to them, they felt that cans were best for chugging the pale-yellow, fizzy, bland mainstream lagers that dominated the market.

Over the past decade, however, attitudes to canned beer have changed. Many microbrewers either have switched from bottles to cans or have begun to package in both bottles and cans. Bottles are expensive to clean and to ship and can easily break or chip. Lightweight cans cool more quickly and, because they are airtight and keep light out, ensure a fresher, unspoiled product. They are popular with hikers and picnickers as they are easy to carry to and from a recreational destination.

At first, the major disadvantage for craft brewers considering switching from bottles to cans was the fact that canning machines were very expensive, and cans, which had to be printed with the label for a specific product, had to be ordered in large quantities. Having made an investment in up to 100,000 cans, a brewer had to commit to making a large volume in the style indicated on the label. Bottles permitted the brewing of smaller quantities and different styles; all that was required was a different label on the bottle. During the last few years, smaller and less expensive canning machines have come on the market, and a method was developed that made it possible to have pre-printed labels affixed to cans. In addition, there are now companies that own mobile canning facilities and travel to smaller breweries where they are able to can as much beer as the brewery or brewpub needs.

But if people want beer fresh from the conditioning tanks, just the way their great-great-grandfathers got it, they may be able to head to a nearby microbrewery or brewpub. They won't have to bring a bucket or pitcher; they can just ask for a growler—a sixty-four ounce, reusable, screw-top glass bottle—or a crowler, a thirty-two ounce aluminum can that can be filled at one of the taprooms and then sealed.

Beer Is Surrounded by Enemies

Beer has many enemies. They aren't legions of keg-smashing temperance zealots; they're light, heat, air, and time. Exposure to light (especially fluorescent light and sunlight) will cause a beer to become light struck and give it a "skunky" flavor. Clear glass bottles are not beer friendly. Brown bottles or (better yet) cans keep the harmful rays away from the liquid. Of course, sun can also warm the beer and make it taste insipid. If it is shelved in non-refrigerated areas at retail outlets or at home, or if it undergoes a series of temperature changes on the way from the store to home, its flavor can be changed for the worse.

Fresh air may be good for people, but it isn't good for beer. When oxygen interacts with it, the result is a stale, cardboard-tasting beverage. If there's too much space between the cap and the liquid level of the bottle, or if the cap isn't fitted tightly, the enemy air may be working on the contents long before you decide to pop the cap.

The final enemy of beer is time. With the exception of some high-alcohol beers such as barley wine, beer has a fairly short lifespan. After three or four months of sitting in the refrigerator or on store shelves, beer should be retired and sent down the sink to its final rest. Check the best-before date if there is one on the label, and, if there isn't, check to see that no dust has gathered on the shoulders of the bottle or the top of the can. A dusty beer is probably an old beer.

When you get home, put your beer quickly into the fridge (making sure that the light is out when the door closes!), and don't save it for a festive occasion that is too far in the future. Don't be fooled by those ads showing a clear-glassed, open bottle of beer that's been set on a table at the edge of a sunlit tropical sea. The weather may be great, but probably the beer isn't.

Enjoying Your Beer

Many people can remember mowing the lawn in the backyard or chopping firewood at the campground or cabin and opening a can of what has been called "lawnmower beer," the stuff that's priced way below the other beers, and chugging it back. It quenches the thirst, and, if it gets warm or is spilt, it doesn't matter, because not only was it really cheap to begin with, but also it probably didn't taste that good. But to enjoy fully a well-brewed lager or ale, it shouldn't be grabbed ice-cold from the refrigerator or the ice chest and gulped from the bottle or can. In the last two decades, aficion-ados have developed a series of steps for enjoying beer that are as intricate as those obsessed over by wine lovers. Enjoying a glass of good beer is a wonderful sensory—some would say aesthetic—experience involving sight, smell, taste, and tactile sensations.

The first thing to remember is that the beer should be served at the proper temperature. Of course, it would be pretty inconvenient and expensive to have several mini-fridges each set at the appropriate serving temperature for a certain style of beer. In her book *Cheese &Beer*, Janet Fletcher offers a very practical method for making sure that the temperature of the beer you are about to pour is just right. Pale ales, IPAs, kolsches, wheat beers, and pilsners should be served straight from the fridge. Amber and red ales, amber lagers, bocks, Oktoberfests, saisons, and sour ales should stand for fifteen minutes after being taken from the refrigerator. Belgian-style strong golden ales, dubbels, and tripels, as well as stouts and porters, should leave the fridge half an hour before they are opened and poured. And barley wine, extra special bitter, and imperial stouts have the longest waiting time—forty-five minutes.

When it's at the appropriate temperature, pour the beer carefully into a very clean, non-chilled glass. An improperly washed glass may contain traces of soap or other residue that can alter the taste of your beer. Glasses chilled in the freezer compartment may have attracted condensed moisture and food odors, and when beer is poured into them, the chill may lower the temperature below the intended serving ranges. If you want to make sure the glass doesn't have any dust in it or hasn't become too warm where it has been standing, fill it with cold tap water, swish the water around inside it, pour the water out, shake the glass to remove any drops, then pour. Do not dry the glass. If you're trying more than one style of beer at a single setting, it's recommended that you use a new glass for each different style of beer.

Different shapes of glasses have been developed to enhance the appearance, aroma, and taste of specific styles. For example, the thin, tapered pilsner glass helps to support the delicate head and to release the carbonation of lagers. The goblet, resting on a thick stem and base, maintains the rich head of stronger Belgian ales. The weizen glass, tapered gracefully outward from the base and then slightly inward, captures the aromas of wheat beers. A brandy snifter is just right for swirling, sniffing, and sipping such high-alcohol brews as barley wine.

There are two schools of thought on how to pour a glass of beer. However, both have the same goals: to avoid spillage, to create a head that's about one inch high, to capture the beer's aromas, and to release the appropriate amount of carbonation. One school advocates pouring the beer into the middle of an upright glass, pausing as often as necessary to prevent the foam from overflowing. The other recommends initially pouring the beer into a tilted glass, then gradually raising the glass to a vertical position to complete the pour.

Once the pour is completed, it's time—not to start drinking but to admire the beer in the glass. Notice its color, the texture of the head, and the bubbles coming from the bottom of the glass. Lift the glass to your nose and enjoy the subtle malt and hop aromas rising from the foam.

Now it's time for the first taste—the most important one, because the palate loses some of its sensitivity with succeeding sips. Take a hearty, rather than a delicate, sip—not an Adam's apple-wobbling, chugalug, "gee, it's hot today" gulp, but enough so that the beer can slide over and along the sides of your tongue on its way to the back of your mouth. The first impressions may be of the malt flavors, usually sweet and, in the case of beers made with darker malts, having notes of coffee or chocolate. The bitterness of the hops usually comes later, counterbalancing the malt's sweetness and often contributing floral or fruity tastes. Depending on the types of hops, malts, and yeasts used, a range of delicate flavors contrasting and complementing each other can be enjoyed in a sip of beer. And if the beer has additives—fruit, spice, or other things nice—taste them as well. They should be delicate and suggestive, not overwhelming.

As your sip is working its way across your mouth, you'll also experience what the beer experts call mouth-feel, the beer's texture. It will range from thin to full-bodied, depending on the style, and maybe more or less effervescent, depending on the level of carbonation. Lagers, especially mainstream ones, tend to be thin-bodied and highly carbonated, the darker ales more robust and frequently not so highly carbonated. Important though it is, the first taste won't tell you everything about the beer you are drinking. With later sips, different characteristics will become evident. Some beers become undrinkable as they get warmer, but others "warm well," revealing new and different flavors and aromas.

If you're having a beer-tasting party, it's recommended that no more than five different beers be sampled; after that, palate fatigue may set in. At a tasting party, provide each guest with a separate glass for each beer to be sampled. (Small juice glasses, wine glasses, special beer sampler glasses, or even small plastic glasses can be used.) Each guest should have a bottle of water and either some bread (such as slices from a white baguette) or plain, unsalted crackers. This food, along with a swig of water, will cleanse the palate between samplings.

For decades, much has been said about pairing wines and foods. Recently beer connoisseurs have stated that beer is a more complex beverage than wine and can be paired with a great variety of foods. It's more than just a beer and a hot dog at the ball game or a beer and a burger in the backyard. Some brewpubs and restaurants have beer cicerones trained to assist patrons in choosing the right beer or beers to accompany whatever menu selections they decide on. Restaurants and brewpubs frequently put on special dinners, with a different beer complementing each course. Three excellent books on food-beer pairing are Janet Fletcher's *Cheese & Beer* (Kansas City: Andrews McMeel Publishing, 2013), Garrett Oliver's *The Brewmaster's Table: Discovering the Pleasures of Real Beer with Real Food* (New York: HarperCollins, 2003), and Julia Herz and Gwen Conley's *Beer Pairing: The Essential Guide from the Pairing Pros* (Minneapolis: Voyageur Press, 2015).

Enjoy the full experience of the beer. And when you're finished, don't forget to wash and rinse the glass thoroughly. Remember, cleanliness may or may not be next to godliness, but full enjoyment of your next beer depends on it.

Appendix 3 - A Guide to Beer Styles

The following guide to beer styles is divided into three sections: lagers, ales, and specialty beers. Following the description of each style are examples that breweries in the Upper Peninsula have made over the last two or three years. (Lack of Upper Peninsula examples after a style definition means that no UP breweries have recently brewed that style.) Because breweries stop producing some beers and add others, some of the examples may no longer available. In putting together the style descriptions, I have drawn on Randy Mosher's *Tasting Beer: An Insider`s Guide to the World`s Greatest Drink* (North Adams, MA: Storey Publishing, 2009), Garrett Oliver`s *The Brewmaster`s Table* (New York: HarperCollins, 2003), and the second edition of Dan Rabin and Carl Forget`s *The Dictionary of Beer and Brewing* (Boulder, CO: Brewers Publications, 2008).

LAGERS

Lagers use bottom-fermenting yeast and are frequently more highly-carbonated and lighter-bodied than most ales. With the development of refrigeration in the later part of the nineteenth century, lagers, which must be brewed and stored at lower temperatures, have become very popular in the United States, where brewers from Germany, the birthplace of most lagers, created versions of the beers of their homeland and established very large breweries and extensive distribution networks. Varieties of North American pale lagers are the most widely-consumed beers in the world.

American Amber Lager: a medium-bodied lager similar to a Vienna Lager.

> Blackrocks Float Copper Amber Lager, Upper Peninsula Deer Camp Amber Lager

Bock: a German-style beer with much fuller and more robust flavors than most other lagers. Lightly-hopped, bocks are dark in color—

from copper to a deep brown—and medium to full-bodied. Doppelbock is stronger in alcoholic content and more full-bodied and darker than bock. It often has chocolate and coffee notes.

ByGeorge Writer's Bock, Cold Iron Jack Frost Doppelbock

California Common Beer: (also called Steam Beer because of the hissing sound made when a keg was tapped) developed in California in the nineteenth century, this beer is amber colored and medium-bodied and is fairly highly hopped. Amber Steam Brewing Company of California has copyrighted the term "steam beer."

Doppelbock: see bock

Dortmunder Export: pale gold in color, with a medium hop bitterness and a crisp finish. The malts contribute biscuit flavors to this medium-bodied beer.

Soo Brewing The Legend Dortmunder

Dunkel: light-to-dark brown in color, this is full-bodied lager with rich, malty flavors.

Ore Dock Six Pointer Munich Dunkel

Helles: from the German word meaning "bright," this medium-bodied beer balances malt and hop flavors. Light straw to golden in color, it often features toasty malt flavors.

Blackrocks Super Deluxe German Helles, Three Bridge Stuttgart German Helles

India Pale Lager: a heavily hopped, quite bitter version of a standard North American lager.

Upper Hand Lumen India Pale Lager

Maibock: a golden-colored bock beer available in the later spring (May). It is distinguished by its sweet, malty notes and relatively light body.

Hereford & Hops Maibock

Marzen/Oktoberfest: brewed in spring and served in the fall, this is a medium to full-bodied, very malty, copper-colored beer with a crisp hop bitterness.

Blackrocks Oktoberfest Marzen, ByGeorge Schultz Beer, Cold Iron Oktoberfest, Hereford & Hops Marzen, Jasper Ridge Marzen/Oktoberfest, Keweenaw Brewing Early Autumn Oktoberfest, Three Bridge Sky Kettle Marzen

North American Lager: pale in color, very light in body, and highly carbonated, with minimal hop and malt flavors.

51st State 3 Vagabonds Light American Lager, ByGeorge Maize 'n' Grace American Light Lager, Cold Iron Porcupine Light Lager, Drifa Lower Harbor American Lager, East Channel Hobo Nectar American Light Lager, LaTulip Light Lager, Tahquamenon Falls Lumber Jack Pale American Lager

Oktoberfest: see Marzen

Pilsner: Bohemian (Czech) Pilsner is a light-bodied and clear, light straw to golden colored beer, with a crispness and spicy tang imparted by the hops. It was originally brewed in Pilsen, where the soft water enhanced the crisp cleanness of the beer. German Pilsner is a light to medium-bodied, straw to gold lager that has spicy hop notes and a slight malt sweetness. It is fuller in body and maltier than Czech Pilsner.

Blackrocks Classic Bohemian Pilsner, Cognition Fjordlands Pilsner, Drifa Silver Skalice Czech Pilsner, Les Cheneaux Buoy Beacon Pilsner, Les Cheneaux Buoy Tipper Blonde Imperial Pilsner, Tahquamenon Falls White Pine Pilsner

Rauchbier: from the German "rauch" for smoke, a dark-colored lager using malt roasted over open fires to impart a smoky flavor.

Schwarzbier: from the German word for "black," a very dark-colored, light-to-medium-bodied beer. The roasted barley malts impart chocolaty flavors that are balanced with a low to medium hop bitterness.

Cognition Desolate Cosmos Schwarzbier , Hereford & Hops Schwarzbier, Keweenaw Brewing Widow Maker Black Beer

Steam Beer: see California Common

Vienna Lager: medium-bodied and reddish-brown to copper, this lager has a malt sweetness balanced with a clean, crisp, but not too strong, hop bitterness. Mexican lagers are often a variation of the Vienna lager style.

Weissenbock: a dark, malty wheat beer with a fairly high alcoholic content.

Other: ByGeorge Ruby's Red Cluster Fugget Red Lager

ALES

Using top fermenting yeast, ales do not require the cooler temperatures for fermenting and conditioning that lagers do, and the brewing cycles are much shorter. Generally speaking, ales are fuller-bodied, darker in color, and richer and more robust in flavor. When the craft brewing movement began in the late 1970s and early 1980s, most craft brewers produced ales, offering beers that were different in taste from lagers made by the megabrewers.

Alt Bier: from the German word meaning "old" (traditional), this copper to brown ale has toasted malty flavors balanced by hop notes that help to create a clean, crisp finish.

> ByGeorge Yooperdorf Alt Bier, Cold Iron Axel's Alt Bier, Drifa Sustadt Alt Bier, Hereford & Hops Alt Bier, Lake Superior October Rust Altbier,

Amber Ale/Red Ale: this copper/red to light brown beer has been called a "darker, fuller-bodied pale ale." It maintains a balance between caramel malt notes and citrusy hop flavors.

> 51st State My Redheaded Cousin American Amber/Red, Brickside Red Metal Amber, Cognition Zombie King Red, Cold Iron Ayer Street Amber, Drifa Never-ending Squawk Amber, East Channel Portside Red, Five Sons Quail's Irish Red, Hereford & Hops Cleary Irish Red, Jasper Ridge Soultaker Red, Keweenaw Brewing Red Jacket Amber, Lake Superior Smokehouse Brewpub Old Foggy Red Ale, LaTulip Irish Red Ale, Les Cheneaux Arborvitae Amber Ale, Les Cheneaux Red Headed Step Child Red Ale, Marquette Harbor Yooper Red Ale, Soo Brewing Maggie's Irish Red, Tahquamenon Falls Tannin American Red Ale, Upper Peninsula Coppertown Amber Ale

American Blonde/Golden Ale: lightly to moderately-hopped, this straw-golden colored blonde beverage is a light-bodied and crisp beer often offered as a "cross-over" beer to newcomers to craft beer.

> Cold Iron Mosaic Blonde, Copper Country Rock Harbor Light, Hereford & Hops Whitetail Golden, Jasper Ridge Wayward Blonde, Keweenaw Brewing Pick Axe Blonde, Lake Superior Backwoods Blonde, Lake Superior Smokehouse Brewpub Golden Blonde, LaTulip Blonde, Marquette Harbor

Blonde, Soo Brewing Laker Gold Blonde, Upper Hand Laughing Fish Northern Golden

American Dark Ale (aka Cascadian Dark Ale/ Black IPA): A American style, this dark brown to black colored beer combines roasty malt flavors with a strong hop presence.

Cold Iron Black River Dark Ale, Keweenaw Brewing Level 92 Black IPA, Lake Superior Smokehouse Brewpub Midnight Black Ale, Les Cheneaux Black Souls Black IPA

American Wheat Ale: a frequently-filtered American version of *hefeweizen*.

Blackrocks Hiawatha American Wheat, Copper Country Gold, Hereford & Hops Soleil Wheat, Jasper Ridge Ropes Golden Wheat, Lake Superior Puddingstone American Wheat, Lake Superior Smokehouse Brewpub American Wheat, Ore Dock Bum's Beach American Wheat, Tahquamenon Falls Harvest Wheat, Tahquamenon Falls Summer Wheat, Tahquamenon Falls Wolverine Wheat, Upper Hand Nowhere Land Wheat, Upper Peninsula Solsken American Wheat Ale

Barley Wine: high in alcoholic content (usually over 10 percent ABV), this has been called a "sipping beer." It is full-bodied and dark brown in color and has complex malt flavors that include caramel, toasty, and fruity notes.

Belgian Blonde/Golden Ale: light to medium-bodied, gold to deep amber in color, this ale has a malty sweetness, spicy notes, and moderate hoppiness.

51st State Winter Torpor Belgian Strong, Ore Dock Blond, Upper Peninsula Golden Gurl Belgian Strong, Upper Peninsula Trail 8 Blonde Ale

Belgian *Dubbel*: a Belgian ale noted for its rich malty flavors and spicy notes. Dark amber to brown, it is lightly hopped. Generally sweet to the taste, with a light to moderate bitterness, it has a dry finish.

Belgian India Pale Ale: see India Pale Ale

Belgian Quad: High in alcoholic content (usually over 10 percent ABV), this dark-colored ale is sweet and malty, with spicy notes.

Belgian Single Ale: often called the Belgian "session ale," this easy-drinking, low alcohol beer is hoppier than most Belgian beers, but has the "funky" yeast flavors characteristic of many of that country's ales.

Belgian *Tripel*: Although lighter in body than Dubbel, this Belgian Ale is stronger in alcoholic content (7 to 10 percent ABV). Bright yellow to gold, it has spicy and fruity notes and a sweetness that is balanced by a moderate hop bitterness.

    Red Jacket Syla Belgian Tripel

***Berliner Weisse*:** crisp, low alcohol (usually under 5 percent ABV) wheat beer, with tart, sour, and citrusy notes

***Biere de Garde*:** meaning "beer to keep," this traditional French ale is a smooth, rich, malt-forward beer, with just enough hops to provide some balance to the malt sweetness. It is, as the name suggests, aged for many months (or even more).

Bitter: The beer that is most often associated with an evening at an English pub, it has a balance between malt sweetness and hop bitterness, with earthy, nutty, and grainy flavors. Light-bodied and gold to copper in color, it is low in carbonation and in alcoholic content (often under 5 percent ABV). ESB (Extra Special Bitter) is more full-bodied and higher in alcoholic content than Bitter. Although it has more bitterness than Bitter, rich malty flavors dominate. Dark gold to copper in color, it is low in carbonation.

    Brickside Jackpine Savage ESB, Five Sons Cheerio English Bitter ESB, Lake Superior Cabin Fever ESB,

Brown Ale: brown ale is noted for its rich malt flavors, including nutty, toffee, and chocolate notes. This medium-bodied beer is generally sweet, although moderate hopping prevents the sweetness from becoming cloying.

    Brickside Quincy Brown, Copper Country Bete Grise Brown, East Channel Harry Bert's Brown, Hereford & Hops Nut Brown, Jasper Ridge Brown, Keweenaw Brewing Lift Bridge Brown, Lake Superior Granite Brown, Red Jacket Our Brown, Soo Brewing 810 Brown, Three Bridge Angler's Brown

Cascadian Dark Ale: see American Dark Ale

Cream Ale: straw to pale gold in color, this light-bodied ale is high in carbonation but low in hop bitterness and has a malty sweetness.

    51st State Never Was Cream Ale, Blackrocks Grand Rabbits Cream Ale, Cognition Bloody Scream Cream Ale, Cognition Deep Scream Cream Ale, Cognition Flower and Dean Cream

Ale, Drifa Pigeon Feathers Cream Ale, Five Sons Honey Ope's Cream Ale, Three Bridge Flirty Mousse Cream Ale

Dark Mild: a popular English session beer which is light to medium-bodied and gold to dark brown in color. Fairly low in alcohol (usually under 5 percent ABV) and in carbonation, it has almost no hop presence. Sweet chocolate and caramel malt flavors dominate.

    Blackrocks Cockney Mild

Dunkelweizen: a wheat beer that uses dark malts and is sweeter than hefeweizen.

    Les Cheneaux Dolomite Dunkelweizen

Extra Special Bitter (ESB): see bitter

Flanders *oud bruin*: this centuries-old Belgian style is light to medium in body and deep copper to brown in color. It is both sweet and spicy. The use of burnt sugar contributes to the sweetness, while the yeasts and such additives as pepper provide spicy notes.

Flanders Red: a Belgian style beer that is light-bodied and red in color. Often barrel-aged for over a year, it is sour and tart and has fruity notes.

Golden Ale: see American Blonde/Golden Ale

Gose: pronounced gos-uh, this low-alcohol German wheat beer is crisp and tart, with salty notes. It is often flavored with fruit additives.

    Cognition The Grace of Faded Things, LaTulip Cucumber
    Sour

Grisette: a light-bodied, low-in-alcohol ale traditionally served to miners in Belgium. It has a creamy mouthfeel, a tangy finish, and nutty notes.

    Barrel+Beam Pret

Gruit: A thousand-year-old style from Western Europe which uses herbs and spices instead of hops for bittering and flavor. Ingredients have included mugwort, bergamot, spruce tips, heather, and wormwood. The modern revival of Gruit is celebrated by Gruit Day, observed annually in early February.

Hefeweizen: from the German words for "yeast" and "wheat," this pale to amber colored ale has been called "liquid bread." Generally close to 50 percent of the malt used is wheat. Highly carbonated, it has virtually no hop character, but does have banana and clove notes. Because it is unfiltered, it has a hazy appearance.

> Brickside Walter's Weizen, ByGeorge Alger Cloudy Hefeweizen, Copper Country White City Hefeweizen, Cold Iron Heat Wave Hefeweizen, Drifa In Irons Hefeweizen, Hereford & Hops Hefeweizen, Keweenaw Brewing Hefe Royale Hefeweizen, Lake Superior Hefeweizen, Three Bridge Never Settle for Weiss Hefeweizen

India Pale Ale (IPA): these pale gold to amber ales are more heavily hopped than are pale ales. In English IPAs, the hop influence is moderated somewhat by the malts, which add bready, caramel notes. American IPAs (sometimes called West Coast IPAs) are much more aggressively hopped, increasing the bitterness and also adding citrusy and floral notes. Double or Imperial IPAs are fuller-bodied, intensely hoppy, and higher in alcoholic content. Session IPAs, a newer version of the style, are lower in alcoholic strength (usually below 5 percent). East Coast IPAs (often called New England, Juicy, or Hazy) have recently been developed and have become increasingly popular. They are hazy in color, have a smooth mouth-feel and little bitterness. Tropical fruit and floral tastes are prevalent. In another recent development, brewers are creating IPAs using a single hop variety, thereby emphasizing the characteristic flavors of that variety. Rye-PAs replace some of the barley malt with malted rye, which adds spicy and tangy notes.

> 51st State On Island Time New England IPA, 51st State Ski Jump American IPA, 51st State Tropical Milkshake New England IPA, Blackrocks 51K American IPA, Blackrocks Frood Noops New England IPA, Blackrocks MyKiss American IPA, Blackrocks Nordskye Session IPA, Brickside Some American IPA, Brickside UP IPA, Brickside Up Hill Both Ways Double IPA, ByGeorge Elephant Disco American IPA, ByGeorge Unicorn Piss New England IPA, Cognition Psybient American

IPA, Cold Iron Drift North American IPA, Copper Country Devil's Washtub Double IPA, Copper Country Miner's American IPA, Copper Country Red Ridge Rye-PA, Drifa Bookseller's Folly Imperial IPA, Drifa Green Ladder American IPA, Drifa Judy's Big Booty New England IPA, East Channel Speedball Tucker New England IPA, East Channel Old Tru's American IPA, Five Sons Alligator Eye-PA English IPA, Hereford & Hops Redemption American IPA, Hereford & Hops Whitewalker English IPA, Jasper Ridge Attack Penguin American IPA, Jasper Ridge Double Frozen Auger Imperial IPA, Jasper Ridge New England IPA, Jasper Ridge WundertDust American IPA, Lake Superior Hindsite American IPA, Lake Superior Southpaw Session IPA, Lake Superior Steelhead Red IPA, Lake Superior Smokehouse Brew Pub Harvey Haze New England IPA, Lake Superior Smokehouse Brewpub Hoppy Days American IPA, LaTulip American IPA, Les Cheneaux Island Hopper Double IPA, Les Cheneaux Northern Tropics Session IPA, Marquette Harbor Lid Back American IPA, Ore Dock Berserker Hazy New England IPA, Ore Dock Reclamation American IPA, Red Jacket Keweenaw Cowboy American IPA, Soo Brewing 13 American IPA, Soo Brewing Huskador New England IPA, Three Bridge Dream Walker American IPA, Three Bridge Excursion Zone American IPA, Three Bridge Inner Earth Double IPA, Three Bridge River Coast Imperial IPA, Upper Hand IPA, Upper Hand Red Buck Red IPA, Upper Peninsula Sunny Dew Hazy New England IPA

Irish Stout: see Stout

Kolsch: originally brewed in Koln, Germany, this beer has been jokingly referred to as "the ale that wishes it were a lager," because of its light body, pale color, and high carbonation. It balances gentle hop and malt flavors and has a crisp mouth feel and a dry finish.

Five Sons Milltown Noble Kolsch, Hereford & Hops Kolsch, Jasper Ridge Copper Kolsch, Lake Superior First Creek Kolsch, Ore Dock Queen City Kolsch

Lambic: this 400-year-old Belgian style ale is unusual in that its fermentation process is natural or spontaneous, using wild yeast that is floating in the air. It has been described as fruity, earthy, sour or tart, and very dry. Gold to amber in color, it is light-bodied and low in carbonation. Unmalted wheat is used in the brewing process. Sometimes brewers will blend old (aged) lambic with young lambic to create a beer called Gueuze, a dry, fruity, effervescent beer. In fruit lambics, whole fruits are added after the start of fermentation and the resulting mixture aged in oak or chestnut barrels. *Kriek* uses cherries; *Framboise,* raspberries, *Peche*, peaches, and *Cassis,* black currants.

Barrel + Beam Spooky Kriek Cherry Lambic

Oenobeer: an experimental beer in which beer wort and grape must are fermented simultaneously. It combines a blend of the flavors of both beer and wine.

Upper Peninsula Rose Eh! Oneobeer

Pale Ale: this gold to amber ale, which was much paler than the popular brown ales and porters of the late eighteenth century, balances nutty, caramel malt notes with a noticeable hop bitterness. English style pale ale is more earthy in flavor as contrasted to West Coast style American pale ale, which has fuller hop bitterness, flavor, and aroma. Both are crisp and have a dry finish. Belgian pale ale is less bitter than the other two and is lighter-bodied and has some malty sweetness. Many brewers are now creating single hop pale ales to highlight the unique characteristics of specific varieties of hops.

51st State State of Superior American Pale Ale, Blackrocks Presque Ale American Pale Ale, Blackrocks Starman American Pale Ale, Brickside Fine Day Pale Ale, ByGeorge Hiawatha Broth American Pale Ale, Cognition Gnome Wrecker Belgian Style Pale Ale, Copper Country Husky American Pale Ale, East Channel Happy Thoughts American Pale Ale, Jasper Ridge Driftwood Pale Ale, Keweenaw Brewing November Gale American Pale Ale, Keweenaw Brewing Point Trail Rye Pale Ale, Lake Superior Sandstone American Pale Ale, Les Cheneaux Navigator American Pale Ale, Marquette Harbor American Pale Ale, Marquette Harbor Chum's Double Pale Ale, Ore Dock Uncle Drew's Flying Machine New England Pale, Red Jacket Smooth Trail American Pale Ale, Soo Brewing English Pale Ale, Tahquamenon Falls Porcupine English Pale Ale, Upper Peninsula Ale, Upper Hand Yooper American Pale Ale, JRA Belgian Pale Ale

Porter: named after the late eighteenth-century London workers for whom it was originally brewed, this brown to black-colored and full-bodied ale uses several malts to create a complex variety of flavors. Relatively low in alcohol, it is moderately bitter. Baltic porters have higher alcohol content.

51st State GC-RA Porter, Brickside Park Bench Porter, Cold Iron Catherine the Great Porter, Jasper Ridge Bonfire Smoked Porter, Ore Dock Porter

Red Ale: see Amber/Red Ale

Sahti: a centuries-old Finnish beer style in which malted and unmalted grains (barley and often rye) are used and the liquid poured over juniper boughs. Wild fermentation provides banana flavors. A cloudy, unfiltered beer, it is fairly high (around 8 percent ABV) in alcoholic content.

Barrel + Beam Sahti, Cognition Sahti

Saison/Farmhouse Ale: designed as a beer with which farm workers could quench their thirst during hot summer days in the fields, this Belgian style ale is gold to amber in color, light to medium-bodied, and highly carbonated. It is spicy (often white pepper is used), moderately bitter, fruity, and sour or tart.

Barrel + Beam Bliss Barrel Aged Saison, Barrel + Beam Partager Saison, Barrel + Beam Heritage Saison, Barrel + Beam Petit Saison, Barrel + Beam Barrel Aged Saison (biere de coupage blend of old and young saison), Barrel + Beam Terre à Terre Saison, Barrel + Beam Terroir Saison, Brickside Farm Beer, Lake Superior Smokehouse Brewpub So Long Saison, LaTulip Farmhouse Ale, Ore Dock Saison, Upper Peninsula Saison

Scotch Ale/Wee Heavy: this strong, dark, creamy, full-bodied ale is mahogany in color. It has caramel flavors and sometimes, because of the malts used, smoky notes.

51st State Woody Wagon Scotch Ale, Blackrocks Barbaric Yawp Barrel Aged Scotch Ale, Cognition Storm to Castle Scotch Ale, Hereford & Hops Highlander Wee Heavy Scotch Ale, Cold Iron Warming Hut Wee Heavy Scotch Ale, Red Jacket Wee Heavy Scotch Ale

Scottish Ale: designated as light, heavy or export depending on the alcoholic content, this ale is not as strong as Scotch Ale. Malt flavors dominate over hops.

Keweenaw Brewing Olde Ore Dock Scottish Ale

Stout: Dark brown to opaque black, it is noted for the roasted flavors imparted by the malted and unmalted barley. English stout is a somewhat sweet ale with caramel and chocolate flavors which are balanced by the hop bitterness. Irish stout is dryer than English versions and often has coffee and chocolate flavors. Designed to be a session beer, it is slightly lighter in body than English versions. Oatmeal stout, in which unmalted oatmeal is added in the brewing process, is very smooth in texture. Russian (Imperial Stout) usually has an alcoholic content above 10 percent ABV. It is not only more bitter than other stouts, it also has much fuller malt flavors.

51st State St. Patrick's Purgatory Irish Dry Stout, Barrel + Beam Acer Barrel Aged Stout, ByGeorge Nighthawk Onyx Beer (dry Irish stout), Cognition Graven-Tosk Gravel Smoked Stout, Cognition Oblivion Milk Stout, Cognition Octopus Was Very Scary Imperial Stout, Cold Iron Sleight American Stout, Copper Country Sturgeon River Dry Stout, Drifa Farmer Queen American Stout, East Channel Lake Street Oatmeal Stout, Five Sons Kraftig Oatmeal Vanilla Stout, Hereford & Hops Blackbird Oatmeal Stout, Hereford & Hops Stumpsitter Stout, Lake Superior Hematite Stout, LaTulip Stout, Les Cheneaux Dark Side of the Brew Stout, Marquette Harbor Stout, Soo Brewing Braveheart Stout, Tahquamenon Falls Black Bear Stout, Three Bridge Tree Shaker Stout, Upper Peninsula Sisu Stout

Witbier: from the Belgian word for "white," this unfiltered wheat beer is pale and cloudy in appearance. Highly carbonated and crisp, it is low to medium-bodied and is often flavored with coriander and orange peel.

Barrel + Beam Blanc Du Nord, Brickside Superior Wit, ByGeorge Snow Pants Romance Wit, Keweenaw Brewing UP Wit Beer, Lake Superior Smokehouse Brewpub Belgian Wit, Les Cheneaux Moon Over Mackinac Witbier, Soo Brewing Grand Cru Belgian Wit

SPECIALTY BEERS

In addition to creating a great variety of styles through their different uses of the four basic ingredients of beer (malts, hops, yeast, and water,) brewers often use such additives as fruits, vegetables, herbs, spices, honey, chocolate, and coffee to introduce nuances of flavor. (In the following list, where the name of a beer does not indicate what additive is used, the additive is named in parentheses.)

Fruit beers: (Note that Belgian fruit lambics are not included in this list.)

51st State Batty Millie Blueberry Wheat Beer, 51st State Coconut Mango IPA, Barrel + Beam Star Plum Barrel Aged Stout, Barrel + Beam Tart Framboise Wheat, By George Blueberry and Maple Pancake Pilsner, ByGeorge Leader of the Patch Strawberry Milkshake IPA, ByGeorge Walking with Giants Apricot Blonde Ale, Cognition Pombluegenesis Kettle Sour Berliner Weisse style Blueberry Beer, Cold Iron Blue Collar Blueberry Kolsch, Copper Country Rice Lake Blueberry Ale, East Channel Island's Grand as Always Blood Orange Hefeweizen, East Channel Paradise Waitin' Blueberry Lager, East Channel Fake News Tart Cherry IPA, Hereford & Hops Blueberry Wheat Ale, Hereford & Hops Choco-Razz Stout (raspberry and chocolate), Jasper Ridge Blastin' Blueberry Wheat Ale, Jasper Ridge Cherry Blonde Ale, Keweenaw Brewing Keweenaw Belle Blueberry Wheat Ale, Keweenaw Brewing Red Ridge Blood Orange Ale, Lake Superior Blueberry Wheat Ale, Lake Superior Smokehouse Brewpub Blueberry Wheat Ale, Les Cheneaux Dingo Blueberry Wit, Marquette Harbor Blueberry Wheat Ale, Marquette Harbor Peach Wheat Ale, Marquette Harbor Tart Cherry Wheat Ale, Ore Dock Blue Canoe Blueberry Berliner Weisse, Ore Dock Bramble on Rose Belgium Golden Strong Ale (raspberries and rose hips), Soo Brewing Crystal Blue Persuasion Blueberry Wheat, Soo Brewing Soo Wheat! Raspberry Wheat Ale, Superior Culture Choco Cherry Brown, Superior Culture Raspberry Chocolate Ale, Superior Culture Wildberry Ginger Beer, Tahquamenon Falls Blueberry Wheat Ale, Tahquamenon Falls Raspberry Wheat Ale, Three Bridge Basic Bitches Blueberry Wheat Ale, Three Bridge Old Fashioned Inspired Winter Ale (cherry concentrate and orange rind), Three Bridge Cranky Dwarf Tart Cherry Sour Ale, Three Bridge Pina Colada Ale (pineapple, coconut), Upper Peninsula Wapatooie! Fruit Beer (mixed fruits), Upper Peninsula Hey Buddy #2 Belgian Wheat Ale with Cranberries

Vegetable beers/ herb and spice:

Drifa Spindrift Ginger Wheat Ale, Five Sons Bee Sting Honey Jalapeno Wheat Beer, Three Bridge Death Candle Pumpkin Pie Ale

Honey/syrup beers:

Blackrocks Honey Lav Wheat Ale, Cold Iron Ice Out Maple Scotch Ale, Cold Iron Drift South Jalapeno American Pale Ale, Cold Iron Michiconsin Honey Cream Ale, East Channel Sapster Maple Double IPA, Les Cheneaux Vera B's Honey Brown Ale, Les Cheneaux Maple Bourbon Barrel-Aged Stout, Les Cheneaux Vanilla Porter, Marquette Harbor Honey Porter, Marquette Harbor Honey Wheat Ale, Superior Culture UP Maple Porter, Tahquamenon Falls Birdseye Maple Ale, Tahquamenon Falls Honey Brown Ale, Three Bridge Flower Hunter American IPA (honey)

Chocolate and coffee beers: (Note that while some malts can impart coffee and chocolate notes to a beer, only those beers which use coffee and chocolate are included in this list.)

51st State Chocolate/Coconut Porter, ByGeorge Big Cups Peanut Butter and Chocolate Porter, Drifa Walk of Shame Coffee Brown Ale, East Channel Uncle Peanut's Peanut and Cocoa Porter, East Channel Widdlestick S'More Coffee Stout, Jasper Ridge Slugworth Chocolate Stout, Keweenaw Brewing Borealis Broo Coffee Amber Ale, Red Jacket Oatmeal Espress Stout (espresso), Soo Brewing Cup of the Day Porter (espresso), Soo Brewing Tiramisu Stout (Chocolate and cappichino), Three Bridge Beno Fino Coffee Stout (with maple syrup), Upper Peninsula Loop-Garou Belgian Stout (chocolate)

Other:

51st State Peanut Butter Cup Stout, Barrel + Beam Arcadian Connection Wild Beer, Blackrocks Coconut Brown Ale, Lake Superior Hazelnut Brown Ale, Superior Culture Birch Beer Blonde Ale, Superior Culture Honey Booch American Pale Ale (with kombucha)

Appendix 4 - Glossary of Brewing Terms

This short list is designed to give brief definitions of some basic terms relating to beer and brewing. More terms and fuller definitions can be found in Dan Rabin and Carl Forget's *Dictionary of Beer and Brewing*, second edition (Boulder, CO: Brewers Publications, 1998), and *The Oxford Companion to Beer*, edited by Garrett Oliver (New York: Oxford University Press, 2011).Descriptions of specific beer styles can be found in Appendix 3.

ABV: Abbreviation for alcohol by volume.

ABW: Abbreviation for alcohol by weight.

additive: An ingredient such as fruit or spices added to the wort during or after the boiling process to add flavors.

adjunct: Corn, rice, or some unmalted cereal grains that are sources of fermentable sugar and can be substituted for malted grain (usually barley) in the brewing process. Beers brewed with adjuncts are usually paler in color and lighter in body. Beer purists complain that megabrewers use adjuncts to cut costs and that the finished products lack taste.

aftertaste: Taste and feel on the tongue after swallowing a mouthful of beer.

alcohol by volume (ABV): Standard mainstream lagers are usually around 5 percent ABV or 4 percent alcohol by weight. Microbrewers often create beers that have higher ABV percentages, although these do not often exceed 10 percent. Occasionally, brewers have created strong (sometimes called extreme or big) beers that have even higher ABV percentages.

alcohol by weight (ABW): Because alcohol weighs less than water, ABW percentages are lower than ABV percentages by approximately 20 percent.

ale: One of the two main categories of beer (the other is lager). Ales are created with top-fermenting yeast (yeast that rises to the top of the wort during the fermentation process). They are fermented at temperatures of between sixty and seventy degrees Fahrenheit and are frequently darker, fuller-bodied, and more robust in flavor than lagers.

all-grain beer: Beer brewed using only malted grains. No malt extracts (syrup made from malt) or adjuncts (such as corn or rice) are used.

barley: The cereal grain that, when malted and mashed to produce fermentable sugars, is one of the main ingredients of beer. The grain comes in two- and six-row varieties, the former being preferred for its higher quality.

barrel: The standard American measurement by volume for beer, a barrel contains just over 31 gallons of beer—that's 55 six-packs of twelve ounce cans.

barrel-aged: Beer that is aged in wooden barrels that previously held such alcoholic beverages as port wine, bourbon, or rum takes on some of the flavors of those liquors, in addition to the flavors of the type of wood with which the barrels are made. Some brewers put barrel staves in conditioning tanks to add flavor.

beer: An alcoholic drink made with the fermented sugars from malted grains, usually barley, and flavored with hops. In Spain, say "*cerveza,*" in France "*bière,*" in Italy "*birra,*" and in Germany and Holland "*bier,*" and you'll derive more enjoyment from your European travels.

body: Sometimes referred to as mouth-feel, it is the tactile sensation—such as thickness or thinness of beer—in the mouth.

bomber: a twenty-two ounce bottle

boutique brewery: Synonym for craft brewery.

Brettanomyces: A strain of yeast often used in traditional Belgian styles, such as lambics and saisons, to give the finished beer "funky" tastes and sourness. Frequently referred to as "brett."

brewpub: A pub that brews its own beer mainly for consumption on the premises, although the beers are sometimes available for takeout in kegs, growlers, bottles, or cans.

bright beer: Beer that, after primary fermentation and filtration and before packaging, is placed in a large tank for clarification, carbonation, and further maturation.

budget beer: Low-priced beer, sometimes referred to by megabreweries as "value-priced" beer and by beer purists as "lawnmower" beer. Frequently, budget beers are brewed with large quantities of less expensive adjuncts (such as corn and rice) replacing malted barley. Many devoted craft beer drinkers drank budget beers as poor college students.

carbonation: The dissolving of carbon dioxide, a by-product of the fermentation process, into beer, creating bubbling and foaming when a bottle is poured or a keg tapped. Beers such as pale lagers, designed to be served at lower temperatures, are more carbonated than those served at higher temperatures. Many drinkers of North American pale lagers are surprised at how relatively "flat" some British ales seem.

cask ale: Beer that undergoes conditioning and secondary fermentation in the vessel (usually a small keg) from which it is served. Frequently, craft breweries or brewpubs hold cask nights that feature small batches of freshly brewed cask ale.

conditioning: A secondary fermentation in which yeast is added after beer has been transferred from fermenting tanks to kegs, casks, or bottles.

contract brewery: A company without brewing facilities that hires another brewery to produce its recipes, but then markets and sells the product itself. This arrangement allows the former to avoid the expense of purchasing equipment and the latter to operate at greater capacity. The term is sometimes used to refer to the brewery that makes the product under contract for another company.

coolship: A large, flat-bottomed, shallow, uncovered tank filled with wort on which wild, airborne yeast acts.

cottage brewery: Synonym for a small craft brewery.

craft brewery: A brewery producing small batches of all-malt (containing no adjuncts) beer.

crossover beer: A beer that is sufficiently similar to mainstream beers to give inexperienced drinkers an introduction to craft beers. Some brewers refer to these as "training wheels" beers. Blonde and golden ales are popular crossover beers.

crowler: A 32-ounce can that is individually filled with beer and sealed at a brewpub or tasting room.

draft beer: A beer, often unpasteurized, that is served directly from a keg or cask. The term "bottled (or canned) draft beer" used by some brewers is an oxymoron.

drinkability: A term frequently used in the advertising of mega-brewers to describe a beverage that tastes good, has a smooth texture, is easy to swallow, is non-threatening, and makes the drinker want another.

dry beer: A beer brewed with yeasts that create a higher alcohol content and which, because there is less sugar in the finished product, is not very sweet and has very little aftertaste.

dry hopping: Adding hops late in the brewing process to enhance flavor and aroma without increasing bitterness.

ester: A compound formed during fermentation that gives fruity aromas and tastes to beer.

extract: A syrupy or sometimes powdered concentration of wort that home brewers often use instead of malted grains.

fermentation: The action of yeast on the sugar in wort, producing carbon dioxide and alcohol. Bottom-fermenting yeasts are used for brewing lagers, top-fermenting yeasts for ales.

fire brewing: Process of using direct fire instead of steam or hot water to boil the wort.

foam: The gathering of bubbles of carbon dioxide at the top of a glass or mug of beer. Aficionados judge the quality of foam by its color, thickness, and retention period. Sometimes referred to as "suds."

gluten-free beer: Beer made without barley or wheat, both of which contain ingredients that can cause people with gluten intolerance to have serious adverse reactions. Rice, sorghum, and corn, which are sources of fermentable sugars, are frequently used as substitutes for barley and wheat.

green beer: Freshly fermented, unconditioned beer. Also, what some people drink too much of on March 17.

growler: A 64 ounce refillable glass bottle used as a beer container by many brewpubs that sell their beer for customers to take off premises.

head: The foam collected at the top of a glass or mug of beer. Also, a part of the anatomy that hurts the morning after a night of excessive imbibing.

hop: The cone-shaped flower of a climbing vine related to cannabis that is used to provide bitterness and a variety of aromas and tastes to beer. Before the development of refrigeration, hops were added as a preservative for ales shipped from England to India. Many varietals of hops used in brewing have been developed in the last fifty years. One of the most important, Cascade, is often an ingredient in India pale ales, the most popular style of the craft brewing "revolution" of the last four decades.

IBU: Abbreviation for International Bitterness Unit.

ice beer: A beer conditioned at temperatures sufficiently low to cause water to form ice crystals, which are then removed to give the beer a higher alcohol content.

imperial: A term often applied to beers with high alcohol content (usually above 7 percent ABV).

International Bitterness Unit (IBU): Unit of measurement, in parts per million, of the level of bitterness contributed to beer by hop compounds. The higher the number of units, the greater the bitterness. The bitterness counteracts sweetness contributed by the malt. Pale North American lagers are low in IBUs (15 or lower), while India pale ales are high (often 60 IBUs or more).

krausening: The process of introducing a small amount of fermenting wort into fully fermented beer to cause secondary fermentation and natural carbonation.

lace: Patterns of foam created on the inside of a glass as the beer level goes down. Beer aficionados consider lacing to be one of the important visual qualities of beer.

lager: From the German word *lagern*, "to store," lager refers to beers that are brewed with bottom-fermenting yeasts and then stored for conditioning for longer periods and at lower temperatures than ales, usually around forty-eight degrees Fahrenheit. Developed in Germany, lager beers became more widely brewed with the development of refrigeration. Now the most consumed type of beer around the world, lagers are the main products of the international megabrewers. Until recently, many craft brewers did not include lagers in their portfolios as the length of the fermentation period tied up tanks for too long.

light beer: A beer that is low in calories and alcohol content, usually 4 percent ABV. Many brewers label these products with the spelling "lite."

light struck: Term applied to beer that has developed an unpleasant, "skunky" taste as a result of exposure to sunlight. In TV ads, beers in clear bottles placed on chairs on the beach look wonderful, but the contents would most certainly be light-struck and taste dreadful.

liquor: A term used by brewers to refer to the water used in making beer. Because the mineral content of water influences the taste of beer, it is important to have the appropriate liquor for the beer style being brewed.

malt: Grain (usually barley) that is soaked in water until germination begins and then heat-dried to convert the starches in it into soluble, fermentable sugars. The length and temperature of the procedure produces different colors of malt that create different flavors and colors in beer.

malt extract: A syrup or powder obtained from the wort. It is sometimes used instead of malt in the brewing process.

Mash tun: An insulated brewing vessel in which the malted grains and water are mixed and heated.

mashing: The process of steeping ground malt in hot water to produce wort, a liquid containing soluble sugars that are converted into alcohol during the fermentation process.

microbrewery: A small brewery with a small annual production, most of which is sold off-premises in kegs, bottles, or cans. The term was a general synonym in the earlier years for all craft breweries, some of which are now very large.

mouth-feel: Texture of beer experienced in the mouth. Beers may be light- to full-bodied and lightly to heavily carbonated.

nanobrewery: A brewery using small brewing equipment, usually of one- or two-barrel capacity, and producing a limited volume of beer annually. Some restaurants have purchased nano-brewing systems so that they can make and serve their own beers.

nitrogen: A gas that, when used instead of carbon dioxide to dispense draft beer, gives the beer a creamy texture. "Nitro beers," in which the beer from a tap or in cans or bottles has been infused with nitrogen, have a smooth, creamy mouth-feel. Nitro beers became popular during the middle of the 2010s.

nose: The aroma of freshly poured beer. Also, a part of the face that may turn red when a person consumes far too much beer at one time.

open fermentation: Putting boiled wort into large open containers so that it can attract wild, airborne yeasts to begin fermentation.

organic beer: Beer made from all or nearly all ingredients that have been certified as organically grown.

pasteurization: The brief exposure of beer to high heat to kill micro-organisms and to extend bottled or canned beer's shelf life. Many craft breweries do not pasteurize their brews, contending that the process adversely affects taste.

pitching: Adding yeast to cooled wort in fermentation tanks to begin the process of fermentation.

publican: A pub or tavern's owner or manager.

real ale: Unpasteurized, cask-conditioned beer served on draft.

Reinheitsgebot: The Bavarian Purity Law, enacted in 1516, which mandated that only barley malt (and, later, other malts), hops, water, and (after it had been identified) yeast could be used to brew beer. Although the German government repealed the law in 1987, many craft breweries still advertise their adherence to the philosophy of the law.

rice: A grain that, because it contains a very high percentage of starch that can be converted into fermentable sugar, is often used as an "adjunct" or substitute for more expensive barley or wheat malts.

saccharification: The process of turning malt starches into fermentable sugars.

scurvy grass ale: According to the *Dictionary of Beer and Brewing*, this was a combination of watercress and ale believed to stave off scurvy. So, if you're planning a solo boat trip across the ocean...

seasonal beer: A beer that is released for a specific season, for example, pumpkin beer in the autumn and bock beer in the spring.

session beer: Because of their low alcoholic levels and smooth mouth-feel, several session beers can be consumed during an evening (a session) at a pub or tavern. Recently, many craft breweries have begun to make session IPAs.

sessionable: term used to refer to beers that are of sufficiently low alcoholic content that a few can be enjoyed "safely" during a "session"

shelf life: The length of time that canned or bottled beer can be kept before beginning to spoil. For most craft beers, this is usually around three months. High-alcohol beer styles such as barley wine may be kept (aged) for considerably longer periods.

SMASH: Acronym for beer brewed with a Single Malt and A Single Hop. Brewers enjoy making these beers to explore different flavors created by the combination of specific varieties/types of the two ingredients.

sour beer: Ales that are given a sourness through the introduction of such bacteria as *Lactobacillus* or *Pediococcus*. Among the better-known styles of sour beers are Berliner weisse, gose, and lambic.

sparging: Hot-water rinsing of mash after the initial separation of mash and wort. The process removes fermentable sugars still remaining in the mash.

special-edition beers: Usually limited, small batches of unusual or experimental styles of beer.

style: A group of beers that share many of the same characteristics of appearance, aroma, taste, and alcohol content. (See Appendix 3 for discussions of specific styles and the names of some of the Upper Peninsula breweries' examples.)

tulipai: The *Dictionary of Beer and Brewing* defines the term as "yellow water" and as a synonym for "tiswin," a beer once brewed by the Apaches. Perhaps it could be used as an alternate word for an impolite term some people use in describing adjunct-laden pale North American lagers.

value-priced beer: Term used by breweries (usually megabreweries) for beers that are priced lower than the other beers they produce. Frequently, value-priced beers use a high proportion of adjuncts. See **budget beer.**

wet hopping: The addition of freshly picked hops during the fermentation process to add flavors and aromas to the beer. Wet-hopped beer is available in the fall, shortly after the hop harvest.

wort: Pronounced "wert," it is the sugar solution created during the mashing process. The solution is boiled with hops, then cooled. Yeast then turns the sugar into alcohol and carbon dioxide.

yeast: The unicellular, microscopic organism that converts sugars in the wort into alcohol and carbon dioxide. Before it was identified, it was considered miraculous and called "Godisgood."

zymology: The scientific study of the processes of fermentation.

Appendix 5 - Reading Ale about It:
A Case of Beer Books

Not only has the number of breweries and brewpubs increased greatly during the first two decades of the twenty-first century, so too has the number of books about beer. Here is an annotated list of twenty-four fairly recent books that I've found entertaining, well-written, and very informative.

Acitelli, Tom. *The Audacity of Hops: The History of America's Craft Beer* Revolution. Rev. ed. Chicago: Chicago Review Press, 2017.

A very thoughtful, detailed history of the craft beer movement in the United States from the middle of the 1960s to the middle of the second decade of the 21st century. Very interesting stories about nearly all the important American craft breweries and brewers of the last half century.

Alworth, Jeff. *The Beer Bible*. New York: Workman Publishing, 2015.

This is an exhaustive, but by no means exhausting, discussion of beer styles, with examples from around the world, written by one of the United States' most respected beer writers. After I've read the chapter about a specific style, I enjoy going to my favourite liquor store to pick up some examples.

Brown, Pete. *Man Walks into a Pub: A Sociable History of Beer*. London: Pan Books, 2003.

One of Great Britain's most popular beer writers presents an entertaining history of the social aspects of the consumption of beer and the places in which it is consumed. The taprooms and brewpubs of the craft beer movement are reintroducing the convivial social aspects of the sipping of suds.

Bueltmann, Fred. *A Rising Tide: Stories from the Michigan Brewers Guild*. Lansing, MI: Michigan Brewers Guild, 2019.

A lively, informal history of the Michigan craft beer movement and of the Michigan Brewers guild. Included are stories about and interviews with Upper Peninsula brewers and owners Derek "Chumley" Anderson, Larry Bell, Andy Langlois, Grant Lyke, and Dave Manson.

Fletcher, Janet. *Cheese & Beer.* Kansas City: Andrews McMeel, 2013.

It's not just a matter anymore of munching Cheezies while gulping down a can of lawnmower beer. Fletcher shows how pairing specific styles of craft beer with specific cheeses brings out the nuanced flavours of each. The photographs are enough to make a person both hungry and thirsty.

Herz, Julia, and Gwen Conley. *Beer Pairing: The Essential Guide from the Pairing Pros.* Minneapolis: Voyageur Press, 2015.

Don't stop with beer-cheese pairings. This book pairs beer styles with a wide variety of foods, including chocolate. There are chapters on organizing beer dinners and on cooking with beer.

Magnaghi, Russell M., *Classic Food and Restaurants of the Upper Peninsula.* Charleston, SC: The History Press, 2022.

The popular Upper Peninsula historian has chronicled the history of the foods and restaurants that have made dining above the bridge a unique culinary experience. Historical photographs include pictures of restaurants that were and some that still are.

Magnaghi, Russell M., *Prohibition in the Upper Peninsula: Booze & Bootleggers on the Border.* Charleston, SC: The History Press, 2017.

A lively account about what Yoopers drank when they weren't supposed to and how they procured what they drank.

Magnaghi, Russell M., *Upper Peninsula Beer: a History of Brewing Above the Bridge.* Charleston, SC: The History Press, 2015.

A history of Yooper beer from earliest times to the craft beer revolution.

Mosher, Randy. Tasting Beer: An Insider's Guide to the World's Greatest Drink. North Adams, MA: Storey Publishing, 2009.

This is a very thorough, frequently quite, but not overwhelmingly,scientific guide. Among the topics covered are "Brewing and the Vocabulary of Beer Flavor," "Sensory Evaluation," beer styles, and beer and food.

Nurin, Tara, *A Woman's Place is in the Brewhouse: A Forgotten History of Alewives, Brewsters, Witches, and CEOs.* Chicago: Chicago Review Press, 2021.

"Don't forget," a friend once told me, "a lot of the early brewers were either monks or mothers." This history celebrates the important role of women from brewery owners to brewhouse workers. I thought about it a lot when, in the summer of my 2022 travels, I met many owners, administrators, and brewers who played important roles in the Upper Peninsula craft beer industry.

Ogle, Maureen. *Ambitious Brew: The Story of American Beer.* Orlando, FL: Harcourt, 2006.

In this compact survey of brewing in the United States from the colonial era to the early years of the craft beer movement, Ogle offers astute commentary on the social and political trends that influenced the making of beer.

Oliver, Garrett. *The Brewmaster's Table: Discovering the Pleasures of Real Beer with Real Food.* New York: HarperCollins, 2003.

One of the rock stars of the craft beer movement, Garrett Oliver is a brewmaster (Brooklyn Brewery), a foodie, and a writer. This is a superbly written book that matches beer styles with complementary food pairings, explaining not only what works, but also why it does.

———, ed. *The Oxford Companion to Beer.* New York: Oxford University Press, 2011.

When I was a graduate student in English, the Oxford literary companions were essential reference books. Now, this one about beer is always close at hand. Hundreds of entries, written by 165 experts, include such topics as breweries, brewing, brewers, ingredients, history, biography, and countries.

Rabin, Dan, and Carl Forget. *Dictionary of Beer and Brewing.* 2nd ed. Boulder, CO: Brewers Publications, 1998.

Over 2,500 terms from *a-acid* (an abbreviation for alpha acid) to *zythum* (an ancient Egyptian name for barley wine).

Rapai, William. *Brewed in Michigan: the New Golden Age of Brewing in the Great Beer State*. Detroit: Wayne State University Press, 2017.

Included in the essays of thirty-two Michigan craft breweries are stories about Ore Dock Brewing and Tahquamenon Falls Brewery.

Revolinski, Kevin. *Michigan's Best Beer Guide*. Holt, MI: Thunder Bay Press, 2013.

This guide, which has profiles of the twelve Upper Peninsula breweries that were operating in 2013, also has light-hearted essays on such subjects as beer commercials, green beer, and home brewing.

Ruschmann, Paul and Maryanne Nasiatka. *Michigan Brewers*. Mechanicsburg, PA: Stackpole Books, 2006.

Written by two veteran beer travellers, this was the first beer guide book devoted exclusively to Michigan breweries. Its profile of individual breweries helps create an historical portrait of the craft beer industry over a decade and a half ago. Stories of the eight Upper Peninsula breweries operating at the time (six are still going strong) are included.

Smith, Gregg. Beer: *A History of Suds and Civilization from Mesopotamia to Microbreweries*. New York: Avon Books, 1995.

Although the focus in its 250 pages is on the United States, there are some chapters about what happened elsewhere and earlier.

Smith, Patti F. *Michigan Beer: a Heady History*. Charleston, SC: The History Press, 2022.

A compact history of Michigan breweries, this book focuses on the pre-craft beer era and includes a chapter on Upper Peninsula breweries.

Stern, Brett. *99 Ways to Open a Beer Bottle Without a Bottle Opener*. San Francisco: Chronicle Books, 2014.

Just in case you need to know.

The Guide to Craft Beer. Boulder, CO: Brewers Publications, 2019.

This pocket-sized little book is full of important information about craft beer. There are short essays, a guide to styles, notes on pairing beer and food, and a tasting log where readers can record their own responses to the brews they have discovered.

Van Wieren, Dale P. *American Breweries II*. West Point, PA: East Coast Brewiana Association, 1995.

A directory, state by state, and within each state, alphabetically by city, of American breweries and their dates of operation from earliest colonial days to 1995.

Webb, Tim and Stephen Beaumont. *The World Atlas of Beer: the Essential Guide to the Beers of the World*. Revised and expanded edition. New York: Sterling Epicure, 2016.

A gorgeous coffee-table book with maps, photographs, and stories about beers from around the world. Even if you can't travel to all of the places covered, you can look, read, dream, and then head to a liquor store with a variety of beers from around the world and, with luck, find a few of the beers discussed.

Acknowledgments

Yooper Ale Trails would not have been possible without the welcome assistance of many people. Thank you to Victor Volkman of Modern History Press who encouraged me to undertake this project and guided me with patience and wisdom along the way. To editor Bob Rich goes my gratitude for his fine work. He not only spotted my many typos but also offered valuable suggestions on ways to improve my writing. To the many brewery owners and brewers, thank you for spending time with me, answering my many questions and generously providing me with "research material" to take back to my little cabin in the big woods. And to my Crooked Lake neighbors, Upper Peninsula friends, and family and friends from afar, thank you for spending golden hours with me sipping on the dock of the bay.

Cheers to you all!

About the Authors

Jon C. Stott (Professor Emeritus of English, University of Alberta) has spent extended summers in the Upper Peninsula for over half a century. He is the author of five beer travel guides, including the award-winning *Island Craft: Your Guide to the Breweries of Vancouver Island*, as well as two other books about Michigan's Upper Peninsula: *Paul Bunyan in Michigan: Yooper Logging, Lore, & Legends* and *Summers at the Lake: Upper Michigan Moments and Memories*. He spends the cold, snowy months in Albuquerque, New Mexico. His beer blog www.beerquestwest.com includes frequent updates on the breweries he has visited.

(photo by Diana Edwards)

Mikel B. Classen has been writing and photographing northern Michigan in newspapers and magazines for over thirty-five years, creating feature articles about the life and culture of Michigan's north country. A journalist, historian, photographer and author with a fascination of the world around him, he enjoys researching and writing about lost stories from the past.   Classen makes his home in the oldest city in Michigan, historic Sault Ste. Marie. At Northern Michigan University, he studied English, history, journalism and photography.

He spent several years living in Grand Marais, MI. While there, he worked at the Lake Superior Brewing Company where he became acquainted with the brewing process of beer. The LSBC was in its early stages and Mikel was able to witness not only its growing process, but that of the beginning of the revival of Upper Peninsula brewing. Learning the ins and outs of stouts, browns, ambers, ESBs, pale ales, and wheats has made Classen perfect for a book like Yooper Ale Trails. He enjoys drinking the stuff too.

Mikel's other books include short story fiction called *Lake Superior Tales*, which won the 2020 U.P. Notable Book Award. *Points North* is a non- fiction travel book published in 2019 which received the Historical Society of Michigan's, "Outstanding Michigan History Publication," along with the 2021 U.P. Notable Book Award. Since then, he has released, *True Tales, the Forgotten History of Michigan's Upper Peninsu*la, and the newest release is *Faces, Places, & Days Gone By, a Pictorial History of Michigan's Upper Peninsula*, published by Modern History Press.

To learn more about Mikel B. Classen and to see more of his work, go to his website at mikelbclassen.com

Index

This index includes the names of breweries and towns with breweries, the names of brewery owners and brewers, and the names of beers brewed in the Upper Peninsula. Beers with "nicknames" are listed by nickname followed by the brewery name in parentheses. Beer with only generic style names (e.g. stout, porter) are listed with the brewery names first.

~ ~ ~

Spend a Summer in the U.P. with Jon C. Stott

Paddling a canoe into sunrise on the longest day of the year... watching a child take her first kayak ride with her father... gazing at a bald eagle, riding air currents high above the lake... chuckling as a hummingbird defends his feeder against intruders... dodging campfire smoke while burning marshmallows and telling scary stories to wide-eyed kids. These are some of the moments and memories depicted in *Summers at the Lake*. The essays-often humorous; sometimes tinged with a sweet melancholy--celebrate the people and events marking the progress of the seasons--from the budding of the first green leaves of May to their falling, gold and scarlet, in September. These prose poems capture the joy of simple, lake-side living and quiet reflection.

"Jon Stott is a masterful storyteller. In *Summers at the Lake*, he shares memories that read like prose poetry. Each story takes us to a place of solitude and beauty and will stir pleasant memories of our own." --Sharon Kennedy, author of *The Sideroad Kids*

"This gentle book by a gentle man is the kind that grows on you. Reading it will give you the same benefits as meditating in lovely surroundings in peace and calmness."
--Bob Rich, author of *From Depression to Contentment*

"In *Summers at the Lake*, much can be learned about life in the U.P. and its enjoyable places. You can explore the wonders of the U.P. while dipping your toes into the everyday experiences of life near Crooked Lake." --Sharon Brunner, *U.P. Book Review*

"Jon C. Stott delightfully describes the many joys of lakeside living with the unchanging activities of summer. Deb Le Blanc's photos will make readers feel as if they are right there at the cabin, next to the author." --Carolyn Wilhelm, MA, *Midwest Book Review*

From Modern History Press

www.ModernHistoryPress.com

Printed in the USA
CPSIA information can be obtained
at www.ICGtesting.com
JSHW081225300124
56279JS00005B/14

9 781615 997275